Raising a Thinking Child

Help Your Young Child
to Resolve Everyday Conflicts
and Get Along with Others

• ◆ • ◆ •

MYRNA B. SHURE, Ph.D.
with Theresa Foy DiGeronimo, M.Ed.

HENRY HOLT AND COMPANY · NEW YORK

Henry Holt and Company, Inc.
Publishers since 1866
115 West 18th Street
New York, New York 10011

Henry Holt ® is a registered
trademark of Henry Holt and Company, Inc.

Copyright © 1994 by Myrna B. Shure, Ph.D.
All rights reserved.
Published in Canada by Fitzhenry & Whiteside Ltd.,
195 Allstate Parkway, Markham, Ontario L3R 4T8.

Library of Congress Cataloging-in-Publication Data
Shure, Myrna B.
Raising a thinking child : help your young child to resolve
everyday conflicts and get along with others / Myrna B. Shure with
Theresa Foy DiGeronimo—1st ed.
p.   cm.
Includes index.
1. Interpersonal conflict in children.   2. Problem solving in
children.   3. Social skills in children.   4. Childrearing.
I. DiGeronimo, Theresa Foy.   II. Title.
BF723.I645S487   1994   94-5166
649'.1—dc20   CIP

ISBN 0-8050-2758-0

Henry Holt books are available for special promotions and
premiums. For details contact: Director, Special Markets.

First Edition—1994

Designed by Victoria Hartman

Illustrations by Herbert W. Wimble IV

Printed in the United States of America
All first editions are printed on acid-free paper.∞

3   5   7   9   10   8   6   4

*To George Spivack,
my friend and
research collaborator
of over twenty-five years*

Contents

Acknowledgments

The research base of the approach for *Raising a Thinking Child* was made possible by grant #MH 20372 (Applied Research Branch) and #MH 40801 (Prevention Research Branch), National Institute of Mental Health, Washington, D.C.

A very special thanks to George Spivack, whose initial research with adolescents demonstrated a critical link between what he called Interpersonal Cognitive Problem Solving (ICPS) skills and behavior. His insights that healthy human functioning and social competence could be guided by problem-solving thinking, and not just by direct modification of behavior itself, led to our joint research efforts to test the theory with younger children—and inspired me to create the interventions that led to the approach developed throughout this book.

Without the help and creative contributions of many people, the formal research, the service delivery, and evaluation of what became ICPS interventions would not have been possible. It was the former administrators of the Philadelphia Get Set Day Care program—Dr. Jeffrey O. Jones, Director; Rosemary Mazzetenta, Assistant Director; Dr. Lafayette Powell, Chief, Psychological Services; and Vivian Ray, Chief Psychologist—who paved the way in 1968 for our very first formal research projects with both teachers and parents of preschoolers. Four Get Set Day Care supervisors deserve recognition for their help in recruiting mothers for that early research: Sarah Bowers, Robert Durso, Sarah Reed, and Phyllis Williams.

Deep appreciation is expressed to Dr. Constance Clayton, former Superintendent, and Leontine D. Scott, Associate Superintendent of School Operations, School District of Philadelphia, for their support of our research in the schools throughout the years. My appreciation also goes to Dr. Irvin J. Farber, former Director of Research in the School District of Philadelphia, for the many times he had to help me problem solve during the research phase of the projects.

I am also indebted to principals of elementary schools throughout the city of Philadelphia who supported our recent research with parents of six- and seven-year-olds, and to the parent coordinators for their efforts in recruiting parents to participate: Blankenburg Elementary School, Dr. Agnes Barksdale, principal, and Vivian Chestang, parent coordinator; W. D. Kelley Elementary School, Mr. Anthony Bellos, principal, and Chantala Clark, parent coordinator; Locke Elementary School, Mrs. Janet Samuels, principal, and Frances Carter, parent coordinator; Martha Washington Elementary School, Dr. Harold Trawick, principal, and Jesse Carter, parent coordinator.

Appreciation and recognition go to Frank Masterpasqua, presently at the Institute for Graduate Clinical Psychology, Widener University, for his invaluable suggestions as project consultant; and to my research assistants—Joan Algeo, Jeanne Handline, and Kathleen Shea—whose insights gained while working with our most recent parent groups helped contribute to the creation of some of the lesson-games adopted for this book. Much insight about helping parents learn ICPS was given to me by Virginia Jamison, an Instructional Support Teacher who, in addition to training teachers in the Philadelphia public school system, also taught ICPS to all the parent-trainers in the more than two hundred schools in the School District of Philadelphia. I am also indebted to Kathryn Healey, now at the Institute for Graduate Clinical Psychology at Widener University, and Phyllis Ditlow, presently education coordinator for the Philadelphia Prekindergarten Head Start program, who help me train teachers and parents around the country. I am always grateful for their original ideas for added flexibility to the program.

Laura Caravello and Dr. Eileen Altman, prevention coordinators of the Mental Health Association in Illinois (MHAI), implemented ICPS for many years with teachers and have now added important insights as they adapt ICPS for parents as well. For their support in this undertaking, I thank Jan Holcomb, Executive Director, MHAI; Ann Nerad, Project Founder and former MHAI board president and member; Dr. Edith Fifer, Administrator for Early Childhood Special Education Programs, Chicago Public Schools; and Dr. James G. Kelly, professor of psychology at the University of Illinois at Chicago and Project Consultant for MHAI. Appreciation also goes to two Chicago public schools for their pioneering ICPS parent training there: Schubert Elementary School, Cynthia Wnek, principal; and Hartigan Elementary School, Betty Greer, principal. I would like to give special recognition to Diane Kacprzak, a Chicago parent who provided leadership to and sparked enthusiasm in other parents in that city. Bonnie Aberson, a school psychologist in Dade County, Florida, has also creatively implemented ICPS for many years with teachers and parents, and it was James Gould, principal of the Calusa Elementary School, who supported the early parent training in that locale.

The games and dialogues illustrated in this book are for use by parents. They can also be used by teachers, counselors, school psychologists, or any school personnel working with

children as a supplement to curricula called I Can Problem
Solve, which I developed for use in classrooms. My gratitude
is expressed to President Ann Wendel and Director of Mar-
keting Russell Pence at Research Press for recognizing the
need to extend the ICPS approach to parents and for allowing
us to reproduce illustrations 2, 3, and 4 and adapt some of the
lesson-games from those classroom manuals.

I thank Lynn Seligman, my agent, for her enthusiastic response to the idea for this book when it was just a seed, and for
finding Theresa DiGeronimo, whose magic touch brought this
book to life—and who, while working on it, became an ICPS
mom herself. And I am deeply grateful to Cynthia Vartan, my
editor at Henry Holt, for believing in this book, for encouraging me, and for making this a very exciting adventure.

Parents of all income levels who participated in pre-training
interviews provided important insights about how unusual the
problem-solving approach is and contributed greatly to the
development of this approach. And those who participated in
the interventions deserve special tribute for their creative and
helpful suggestions that led to the refinement of problem-
solving techniques for raising a thinking child. But it was that
disarming troupe of critics, ages four to seven, who provoked
us into constant change. It is to them I owe the greatest tribute
of all.

—MBS

Introduction

This is a book about childrearing—but it will not tell you what your children should do or how they should behave. Instead, it will show how you can affect your children's social adjustment by encouraging them to think. I'm talking about a very special kind of thinking—the kind involved in solving everyday problems that come up with others. This book is about a research-based, clinically proven, child-tested approach called I Can Problem Solve, or ICPS for short.

Think of a problem you had recently with a spouse, a co-worker, a friend, your child—anyone, really. Think about how you felt before the problem was resolved—anxious, worried, angry, frustrated? Now think about how you felt after the problem was solved—relieved, happy, proud? Imagine if problem after problem remained unresolved. How might that begin to affect how you feel—and what you might do—over time? Perhaps you might feel inadequate and helpless and begin to act out in socially unacceptable ways. This is how children feel when they can't successfully resolve problems that come up with other people.

Of course, people of all ages have problems that center on typical, everyday kinds of conflicts and unsatisfied needs and/or desires. That's natural. While you may want a neighbor to quiet down at night, an adolescent may want an unobtainable date, and a four-year-old may cry for a toy he can't have. What's different about all these "wants" is how each person tries to obtain them. I have discovered that people who can think in a problem-solving way are more likely to find success and are better adjusted socially than those who cannot think that way, or who haven't yet learned to.

On a radio talk show I do in Philadelphia, I interviewed some parents who were beginning to prepare their high-school-age daughter for college. These parents believed it was important to start teaching their daughter decision-making skills now, before she left home. I told them how I could help children learn decision-making skills and how to think for themselves much earlier than in high school. They were surprised to find they could have begun this when their daughter was three or four years old. One ICPS mother, for example, helped her four-year-old son, Robert, decide how to persuade his friend to let him play with his toy. When Robert said he could just grab it, his mom helped him think about that solution. She helped him consider how he and the other child might feel, what might happen next, and what else he could do. This kind of talk, called "ICPS dialoguing," helped Robert become a better problem solver. Even though he is only four years old, Robert has already begun to think for himself.

Why is Robert's new ability to think so important both for himself and for his parents? With George Spivack, my research colleague of more than twenty-five years, I have learned that youngsters who can recognize that behavior has causes and consequences, that people have feelings, and that there is more than one way to solve everyday problems that arise with others have fewer behavior problems than those who merely react to the problem at hand.

Through careful evaluation of thousands of youngsters nationwide, my fellow researchers and I have learned that ICPS-competent children are less easily frustrated, less likely to fly off the handle when things don't go their way, less aggressive, and also more caring about others, more likely to share and take turns, and better able to make friends. Some overly withdrawn youngsters learn to stand up for their rights and become more outgoing.

With our earliest research showing a distinct association between problem-solving thinking and behavior, we asked: If these kinds of thinking skills distinguish children who do and do not display socially competent behaviors in school, can we help low-ability problem solvers learn these skills, and would learning them bring them up to the level of their more competent age-mates? If gains in problem-solving thinking skills indeed guide behavior, then we would be able to offer a new approach to reducing and possibly preventing problem behaviors before they get out of control.

I started with six youngsters in a nursery school. I listened to them carefully as I tried to teach them concepts that I thought would help them learn to problem solve. I noticed that when I asked the group for a "different" idea to solve a hypothetical problem that I presented, I kept hearing the same solution over and over. Some of the children really could think of only one or two ways. Others, I discovered, did not understand the meaning of the word *different*. Whether or not they knew the meaning of the word, I realized that playing with that and other early word concepts could set the stage for later problem-solving thinking. I made up games using some key words. Playing with the word *different* would ring a fun bell of association from the games when I then asked them for a "different" way to solve the problem. Playing with the word *not* would help them associate the games with the question "Is that idea a good idea or is it *not* a good idea?" The simple two-letter word *or* is a word for the longer word "alternatives" that preschoolers could understand so they could later think,

"I could do this *or* I could do that." After several pilot trials with children, I then trained four teachers, then ten, and slowly built up to hundreds more over the years.

At first the skills of alternative solution and consequential thinking were called Interpersonal Cognitive Problem Solving, or ICPS skills—too much of a mouthful, I thought. Lying in bed one night, it came to me. The initials *ICPS* can mean, "I Can Problem Solve." And the very first day this was introduced, one boy hit another, and the victim said loud and clear, "He's not ICPSing." My approach had a name.

What did we learn from our research? First, youngsters exposed to ICPS in preschool improved in their problem-solving abilities more than a comparable group tested but not trained. Second, those youngsters who improved in the ICPS skills were the most likely to show a decrease in both impulsive and inhibited behavior, and these gains lasted when measured one and two years later. Third, preschoolers not showing behavioral difficulties were less likely to begin showing them in kindergarten if they were exposed to ICPS. (This is very important because it suggested that no matter how good a child was at solving problems, he or she could get still better, perhaps because a style of thought that includes such flexibility is likely to be perpetuated.)

Given the highly positive results of our efforts, we took our program to the home. I completely readapted it for use with a single child at home (although parents can also use the approach with more than one child). We learned that not only could parents impart the program successfully to their children at home, but as rated by their teachers in school, the children took their newly acquired thinking skills and used them at school, too.

Our newest research is showing that in addition to behavior changes, as early as grade one, ICPS-trained children do better in their academic curriculum as well. It is possible that once behaviors mediated through ICPS skills improve, youngsters can better absorb the task-oriented demands of the classroom, and subsequently do better in school.

Indeed, children who learn how to think about their relationships with other people do better in life in general. Consider for a moment the people in your circle of family, friends, and co-workers who are most often unhappy, agitated, depressed, or even violent:

- the mothers or fathers who resort to verbal or physical abuse when they're frustrated by their children's disobedience
- the couples who divorce because they can't compromise
- the teens who abuse drugs and alcohol because they can't resist peer pressure
- the young man who responds to frustration with violent or self-destructive behavior

It's a good bet that these people have never learned to deal thoughtfully with other people in problem situations.

Now consider the unhappy young children also struggling to fit into the world outside themselves:

- the angry preschooler who bites her friend because she wants her toy back
- the demanding five-year-old who whines, cries, and nags when his parents can't give in to his demands immediately
- the shy six-year-old who withdraws because she often gets picked on by her more outgoing classmates

Our research, supported by others described by Spivack and Shure in "Interpersonal Cognitive Problem-Solving and Clinical Theory," has shown that if children can learn to solve typical everyday problems, they are less likely to become impulsive, insensitive, withdrawn, aggressive, or antisocial. It's so crucial to nip these behaviors in the bud because, according to Parker and Asher in "Peer Relations and Later Personal Adjustment," they have been known to lead to more serious problems later—problems such as psychopathology, substance abuse, delinquency, teenage pregnancy, or academic failure, and even, as we witnessed during the Los Angeles riots, extremely violent and antisocial behavior. Overly withdrawn children, according to Cheek et al. in "Adolescent Shyness," have potential for later loneliness, low self-esteem, and depression.

Although educators and clinicians historically have asserted that relief of emotional tension can help one think straight, ICPS supports the reverse idea—the ability to think straight can help relieve emotional tension. Quite clearly, in the long run it is important for children to learn how to think about the problems they encounter in their dealings with other people.

I believe that as you use ICPS, you will find that the approach offers immediate benefits to both you and your child. ICPS will help *you:*

- increase your awareness that your child's view may differ from your own;
- see that helping your child think a problem through may in the long run help more than immediate action to stop what she is doing;
- provide a model of problem-solving thinking for your children—as a thinking parent, you might inspire your child to think.

ICPS will help your *children:*

- think about what to do when they face a problem with another person;
- think about different ways to solve the same problem;

- think about the consequences of what they do;
- decide whether or not an idea is a good one;
- realize that other people have feelings and think about their own feelings too.

Although very different from other popular methods of parenting, the ICPS approach continues the movement toward positive childrearing. In 1965 Haim Ginott sparked interest in positive parenting by suggesting in his book, *Between Parent and Child,* that instead of telling a child what *not* to do ("Don't run!"), parents should emphasize the positive by telling them what *to* do ("Walk!"). Then, in 1970, Thomas Gordon wrote the acclaimed book *Parent Effectiveness Training* (PET), which opened the door to the idea that active listening and using "I" messages ("I feel angry when your room is messy") instead of "you" messages ("You are too messy") are learned parenting skills. These two landmark books paved the way for *Raising a Thinking Child* to take parents a step further. ICPS moves from a primary focus on skills of the parent to focus on skills of the child as well. The thinking child does not have to be told how people feel or what to do; the thinking child can appreciate how people feel, decide what to do, and evaluate whether the idea is or is not a good one.

For twenty-five years, ICPS has proven successful through careful evaluation of thousands of ICPS-trained youngsters up to age twelve with varied IQ levels from urban and suburban schools nationwide, including Delaware, Florida, Illinois, New Jersey, Ohio, Oregon, Pennsylvania, Tennessee, Utah, and Virginia. This approach to problem solving has been documented in three books for professional audiences, in educational training manuals, and in numerous articles in professional journals. It has also received several national awards: In 1982 ICPS was chosen by the National Mental Health Association to receive the prestigious Lela Rowland Prevention Award, and in 1984 my research colleague, George Spivack, and I received the Award for Distinguished Contribution to Community Psychology, sponsored by the Division of Community Psychology of the American Psychological Association. In 1987 ICPS was selected as a model mental health prevention program by the Task Force on Promotion, Prevention, and Intervention Alternatives, sponsored by the American Psychological Association. In 1992 the National Mental Health Association selected ICPS as one of its recommended programs; as a result, the mental health associations of Illinois, Alabama, and Georgia have selected it as their model program, with Georgia offering ICPS training to its representatives from key local centers across the entire state. Most recently, in 1993, the special task force on model programs, Division of Clinical Psychology Section, Child Psychology, and the Division of Child, Youth, and Family Services of the American Psychological Association also chose ICPS as a model prevention program nationwide.

Raising a Thinking Child is based upon our research and practical experiences with parents of children up to age seven. I have come to appreciate how unusual the problem-solving approach is. I have also come to appreciate how easy it is for parents to teach interpersonal problem-solving skills to their children at home—and now I offer ICPS to you.

Myrna B. Shure, Ph.D.

• ◆ • ◆ •

PART I

Helping Your Child Think About Problems

1

♦ ● ♦

How to Think,
Not What to Think

What do you do when your child nags, demands, or cries?

How do you react when your child hits other children or takes away their toys?

What do you say when your child won't listen to you or do what you ask?

You probably react to these kinds of behaviors in a variety of ways. You may model or coach more acceptable ways to behave. Sometimes, you might choose to ignore the problem. Other days you might tell your children what to do and what not to do, and even explain why. When I was a nursery school teacher, I tried all of these things. Most of the time, none of them worked. I believe now that these methods were not successful for a very simple reason: I was doing the thinking for the child. All of us like to be free to think for ourselves. And, I have learned, so do young children—if they have the skills to do that.

Through the pages of this book, you'll see that my view of promoting healthy and responsible behavior goes beyond just what we *do*. It gives at least equal weight to how we *think,* because how we think affects what we do. My approach introduces problem solving to children. Its most important feature is that children are not taught what to think or do, but *how* to think so they can decide for themselves what and what not to do, and why. I'll be talking about a very unique kind of thinking that helps solve typical, everyday problems that affect how children deal with other people. And I'll show you how even very young children can learn to solve their own people-problems; they learn to do this by practicing a series of thinking skills from a program I call ICPS—I Can Problem Solve.

Meet an ICPS Family

The family we'll follow throughout this book as they move through each stage of the ICPS approach is a composite of real families I've worked with over the years, of real episodes, and of real dialogues. It is not uncommon for children in the same family to differ in their problem-solving ability. Due to a combination of factors, which often include past experiences, parental discipline styles, and the child's temperament, children do differ dramatically in their ability or tendency to think through their problems. The family you will come to know is a good example of these differences.

◆　◆　◆

First, I'd like you to meet four-year-old Alex. Before his mother began ICPS with her children, Alex was an impulsive and sometimes aggressive boy who was not very good at solving his own problems. He was unable to consider how other people might feel about his actions and he had a hard time sharing or taking turns. Alex often resorted to kicking or grabbing for what he wanted and he didn't seem to care that these solutions usually got him into trouble. While many children Alex's age are already good problem solvers, Alex was not one of these children.

For example, one day at nursery school Alex shared his magnets with his classmate Jonathan, but then wanted them back. When Jonathan refused his request, Alex tried to grab them. Jonathan answered with a good swift kick and they started to fight. Alex, red with frustration, began to scream and kick more violently. Jonathan became frightened and retreated, so Alex got what he wanted.

When Alex was denied his wish, his inability to think of another solution to his problem created intense distress and anger. The possibility of getting into a fight did not stop him because he could not (or would not) think of anything else to do. He was probably much more concerned about what would work "now" than about what might happen later.

On the other hand, Alex's sister, six-year-old Alison, responded to problems with her friends in a different way because she was already a good problem solver. For instance, one day Alison wanted something her classmate Melissa had. In an after-school play group, she asked Melissa to give her a cup containing plant seeds. When Melissa said, "No, I need the seeds," Alison didn't create a new problem by reacting impulsively. Her ability to think of other options led her to try another approach. "When I get the big bike, I'll let you ride it," she said. Defiantly, Melissa shouted, "I said *no!*" Alison then asked, "What are you going to do with those seeds?" And Melissa answered, "Grow them." A few minutes later, Alison returned with a sand shovel and offered, "I'll bury some and you bury some. Two of

ers can be yours and two can be mine. How's that?" Melissa
and Alison began to count the seeds, each burying "their
own" in the dirt.

Alison has a lot in common with other good problem solvers. When her first solution to get the cup of seeds didn't work,
she tried another way. But that didn't work either. Alison then
found out that Melissa had a reason not to share because she
was going to "grow the seeds." This opened the door for
Alison to suggest her idea that each bury some. She might have
thought about yelling and screaming or grabbing the cup, and
she may also have thought about starting a fight. But most
important, in the end, Alison was able to think how to mesh
her needs with those of Melissa's and to think of other options.
This kind of thinking prevented Alison from experiencing frustration and failure.

Our extensive research over the years suggests that from as
early as age four, sometimes even three, good problem solvers can bounce back and think of other ways to get the
things they want, and they can better cope with the frustration when they cannot have what they want. When they're
stymied, they can find different things to do, and, as a result,
their mothers do not have to tell them what to do—they can
think for themselves. This makes children not only less nagging and demanding of others, but others less nagging and
demanding of them.

This is the goal of ICPS: to teach these problem-solving
skills to children who are now poor problem solvers and to
encourage the continued growth of these skills in children who
show early signs of proficient problem-solving techniques.
Even good problem solvers can become better and can turn
their natural inclination into problem-solving habits that can
prevent later interpersonal conflicts.

To illustrate how you can teach your children ICPS skills,

we will follow Alex and Alison as they learn, practice, and use this style of problem solving. We will see how their two-year-old brother, Peter, joins in on the early games. We'll also meet Alison's friend Tanya. Tanya's mother learns how this approach to problem solving can help her child, who feels shy when away from home, become less timid and fearful of other kids. We'll see how ICPS builds Tanya's sense of social competence, allowing her to jump into play with other children. Through the experiences of these children, we'll see how a child's thinking skills are shaped through the repetition of key problem-solving words, sensitivity to their own and others' feelings, the generation of alternative solutions, and the consideration of consequences.

In the end, we'll see how this kind of thought process encourages children to think for themselves when they face problems with other people.

When Marie, Alex and Alison's mother, began using ICPS with her family, the idea of letting her children think for themselves made her worry that they wouldn't think of "correct" solutions. Their father, who joined in ICPS after he saw how it worked, agreed. I told them, as I've told other parents with a similar concern, that the emphasis of the ICPS problem-solving approach is not always on "correctly" solving the problem now, but on helping the child practice thinking about the problem-solving process so he or she can deal with new problems when they come up in the future. This emphasis is important because if you continually *tell* children what to do, they have no opportunity to think about and explore other options.

Let's look at how Alex's mom talked to him before beginning ICPS. Alex had brought his own magnets to school and then ran into trouble when he grabbed them back from his friend Jonathan. (You may find these explanations similar to those you might use yourself.):

MOM: Alex, your teacher tells me you grabbed toys again. Why did you do that?

ALEX: 'Cause it was my turn.

MOM: You should either play together or take turns. Grabbing is not nice.

ALEX: But they're mine!

MOM: You must learn to share your toys. You can't bring them to school if you're not going to share them. Jonathan was angry and he won't be your friend.

ALEX: But Mom, he wouldn't give them to me.

MOM: You can't go around grabbing things. Would you like it if he did that to you?

ALEX: No.

MOM: Tomorrow, you tell him you're sorry.

In this verbal exchange, Alex's mom certainly didn't give him any room to choose a "wrong" solution. She asked him why he grabbed the toy, but then didn't listen to his answer. She explained the consequences of his actions, and then told him what to do—first to share, and then to say he's sorry. Alex's mom was so intent on teaching her child to share that she did all the thinking and talking.

In my work with children using ICPS, I've learned that, given the skills and the opportunity, children trained to problem solve chose the "wrong" solution quite infrequently because ICPS parents approach the problem differently. They teach their children a set of thinking skills that help them to identify the problem, see how they and others might feel as a result of their actions, anticipate what might happen next, and recognize that there is more than one way to solve the problem. When children learn to do this, I have learned that they generally do choose a solution that has fewer negative consequences for themselves and for others.

One End Product

Let's see how Alex's mother helped her son think about the grabbing-the-toy problem after she became an ICPS mom.

MOM: Alex, your teacher tells me you're grabbing toys again. Tell me what happened.
> (*Mom helps child identify the problem.*)

ALEX: Jonathan had my magnets. He wouldn't give them back.
MOM: Why did you have to have them back right then?
> (*Mom gets more information.*)

ALEX: 'Cause he had a long turn.

Alex's mother just learned something she did not discover when she simply demanded he share. She learned that from her son's point of view, he had shared his toy. The nature of the problem now seemed different. The dialogue continued.

MOM: How do you think Jonathan feels when you grab toys like that?
> (*Mom helps child think about the other child's feelings.*)

ALEX: Mad, but I don't care; they're mine.
MOM: What did Jonathan do when you grabbed them?
> (*Mom helps child think about the
> consequences of his act.*)

ALEX: He hit me.
MOM: How did that make you feel?
> (*Mom helps child think about his feelings too.*)

ALEX: Mad.
MOM: You're mad and your friend is mad, and he hit you. Can

you think of a different way to get your toy back so you both won't be mad and so Jonathan will not hit you?

ALEX: I could ask him.

MOM: And what might happen then?
(Mom guides child to think of consequences
to positive solutions too.)

ALEX: He'll say no.

MOM: He might say no. What else can you think of doing to get your toy back?
(Staying focused on the child's problem, Mom
encourages him to think of more solutions.)

ALEX: I could let him play with my toy cars.

MOM: Good thinking. You thought of two different ways.

This time Alex's mother did not try to solve the problem the "right" way from her point of view. She did not tell her son to share or even explain why he shouldn't grab. In fact, when she asked Alex why he had to have the toy back right then, the focus shifted from Alex's grabbing as the problem to his grabbing as the solution to a different problem—how he could get his toy *back.*

Alex's mom helped him think about his own and others' feelings, the consequences of his act, and what else he could do. This mother was teaching her child *how,* but not *what,* to think. She was using a problem-solving style of talk—a style I call ICPS dialoguing.

I know you must often feel your children don't listen to you, but the first dialogue between Alex and his mother shows that children must often feel that no one listens to them either. When the child is trying to solve one problem (in this case, "I did share; now I want my toy back"), and the mother is trying to solve another ("My child must learn to share"), it seems that telling, demanding, even explaining ends up in frustration for both. Although Alex won't be able to verbalize it directly, he now begins to sense that "someone cares how I feel. Someone cares what I think."

This example illustrates a complete ICPS dialogue that includes the full range of thinking steps. Even this extended version takes no longer to deliver than it does to argue, debate, or give long explanations that often fall on deaf ears anyway. Even so, after using the full-length dialogues for a while, most parents I've worked with have found that they didn't have to go through all the steps all the time. On one occasion when Alex hit his friend, all his mom had to ask was, "Is that a good idea?" "Can you think of a different way to solve your problem?" This quick reminder dialogue was enough to help Alex think of another, more positive way to solve his problem.

How did Alex and his mom get to this point? Let's move on to the next chapter and see how it all began.

2

◆ ● ◆

Playing with Words

Talking in ways that help children think through their problems is what ICPS is all about. In this chapter we'll discuss six of the word pairs that form the basis of ICPS dialogues: IS/IS NOT, AND/OR, SOME/ALL, BEFORE/AFTER, NOW/ LATER, SAME/DIFFERENT.

Although your child may already be familiar with all or most of these words, they are used in a special way with ICPS and are introduced in gamelike activities throughout this book. Your children will laugh when you first say, "Mommy IS a lady but she is NOT a kitten." And, "Our feet look the SAME, but your feet are a DIFFERENT size." Or perhaps even, "Do you think I should eat this banana BEFORE or AFTER I peel it?"

These words are used in game form because when children learn to associate particular words with play, they are more likely to use them when it's time to settle disputes. For instance, these word pairs help children think if an idea *is* or *is not* a good one, and to think about what happened *before* a fight began, and whether "he hit you BEFORE or AFTER you hit him." Children enjoy thinking about different ways to solve their problem when they associate the word *different* with fun. And they're more willing to wait until later when they recognize the word *later* from their play games.

Introducing Problem-Solving Words

The way Marie introduced ICPS vocabulary words to her children will give you an idea of how you can teach problem-solving words in your home. But feel free to make up your own games and follow your child's lead as you begin to use each word pair.

Marie decided to introduce ICPS to her four-year-old, Alex, during the day when Alison was in school. (Alex seemed more attentive when Alison wasn't around, and Marie knew Alex would like the idea of telling his sister about ICPS later in the day.) "Once in a while, we're going to play a game called I Can Problem Solve," she said. Alex was always happy to have some time with his mom, so he liked the idea right away.

"These games will help you have more fun when you play with Alison and your friends," Mom continued. "They'll help you think of ways to get Alison to let you play with her toys, to get her to leave you alone, and to solve your own problems without calling me. Doesn't that sound like a good idea?"

Alex agreed, "Let's play!"

Is/Is Not

The word pair IS/IS NOT is quite easy for four-year-olds like Alex to understand. Even two-year-old Peter will be able to join in.

"I'll go first: Alex IS a boy; he is NOT a balloon. Right?" asked Marie, emphasizing the ICPS words.

Alex laughed.

"What else is Alex NOT? Alex is NOT . . ."

"I'm NOT a house!" giggled Alex.

"That's right. What else are you NOT?"

"I'm NOT a . . . bunny."

"I'm NOT a bunny," repeated Peter.

"I'm NOT a . . . fish," said Alex.

"I'm NOT a fish, too," laughed Peter.

"I'm NOT a . . . telephone pole!" exclaimed Alex.

And so the first try with ICPS games got off to a good start. So good that Alex didn't want to stop; he romped around the living room pointing to one thing after another shouting, "This is NOT a butterfly." "This is NOT a truck." "This is NOT a bug." Marie was delighted to watch his enthusiasm and found that these word games were easy to play anywhere, anytime.

And/Or

In the grocery store later that day, Alex and his mom continued IS/IS NOT games and added AND/OR games. The words *and* and *or* are concepts we use when we want to think about more than one way to solve problems.

"This IS an orange," she stated. "It's NOT ice cream."

Alex lit up when he recognized the words of the ICPS game. "It's NOT a . . . toy, too!" he jumped in.

"That's right. Now let's see, should I buy the oranges OR the apples? OR should I buy the oranges AND the apples?"

"Yeah, Mommy. Buy the apples AND the oranges."

"Okay, but I have to pick only one kind of juice. Should I buy grapefruit juice OR cranberry juice?"

"Buy both!"

"No. Today I have to choose this one OR this one."

Alex began to yell at his mother. "No. I want both! Buy both!"

"Alex, listen to the game," insisted his mother, trying to get his attention. "You can tell me if grapefruit juice IS or is NOT the one you want. Go ahead."

The familiar sound of the ICPS words seemed to help Alex calm his tantrum. Still pouting, but much calmer, he hit the carton of grapefruit juice, saying, "This is NOT the one I want."

"Good. You decided which one you want. Let's buy the cranberry juice."

Marie hoped that familiarity with ICPS words *or* and *and* would later help her children think of many possible solutions to their problems rather than jumping at the first impulsive one that comes to mind.

Finding Time for ICPS

Playing these games during her daily routine showed Marie that she needn't worry anymore about one of her original concerns. When first introduced to ICPS, Marie said to me, "I don't have time to start any kind of organized teaching program with my children." I was happy to tell her that one of the most practical features of the ICPS approach to teaching problem solving is its flexibility. ICPS begins with word games that can be played anywhere—in the car, in the supermarket, at the dinner table, during play- or story time—anywhere you and your children are normally together. The game concepts are then transferred to dialogues that you use when your children face problem situations—the kind common in every household: hurting playmates, whining for attention, interrupting your conversations, misbehaving in school, fighting with siblings, and the like.

There is nothing formal, mandatory, or time-consuming about ICPS dialogues. They have been made to be used within your normal, everyday routine. This was most important to Marie because, as she says, "I don't have time to be a supermom." Right from the start, Marie told me, "To be perfectly honest, if I get my kids up and dressed and fed on time, my morning's a success. Then after school, we start juggling my job with their scout meetings, sports practices, and my grocery shopping; then we move on to homework, supper, baths, and bed. Can ICPS fit into that kind of schedule?"

You'll see as we move through the program that ICPS can fit into even the most hectic schedule. You can, if you like, make special time for games and activities, but you can also weave them right into your daily routine.

Playing More Word Games

That night Alex wanted to tell Alison about his new game.

"Ma!" yelled Alex. "Tell Alison about the IS/IS NOT game."

"It's called," said Mom, laughing, "the I-Can-Problem-Solve game. Let's call it ICPS for short."

"How do you play it?" asked Alison curiously.

"Well, it starts out as a word game," said Mom. "Here, let's use Peter's storybook to show you. Look at this picture of Mary and her little lamb. Peter, tell me which picture IS the lamb?"

When Peter pointed to the lamb, Mom praised him and continued. "Good. Now, Alex, tell me: IS that lamb allowed at school or is he NOT allowed?"

"He's NOT," yelled Alex.

"Right. Now point to the girl AND the lamb."

Alex pointed.

"Good. Now point to the picture of the girl OR the lamb."

Alex pointed and turned his proud smile to Alison.

"That's too easy," Alison said as she started to walk away.

"Wait," said Mom. "Try this, Alison. Look at the picture and tell me: Is Mary wearing a dress AND a hat, OR a dress but NOT a hat?"

After thinking about her choices, Alison looked at her mom, annoyed. "What do you mean?"

"Take your time and decide if Mary is wearing a dress AND a hat, OR a dress but NOT a hat."

"She's wearing a dress AND a hat."

"Right. See, if you think carefully about the question, you can pick the right answer. How about this: Is the lamb standing by Mary AND the school, OR by Mary but NOT the school?"

This time Alison answered more quickly "He's standing by Mary AND the school."

Alison's mom changed the complexity of her questions for Alison because the game has to be fun and it should make children think before answering. Familiarity with these words will allow children to think before trying to solve problems. They'll learn to consider options by saying, "I can solve this problem by doing this OR that. Maybe I can do this AND that. I think I'll do this but NOT that."

Alex had grown impatient listening to Alison play the game and soon stood up and screamed at his mother, saying, "It's *my* turn."

"Alex, IS that a good way to ask for a turn, OR is that NOT a good way?"

With a smile of recognition, Alex admitted it was NOT a good way.

"Well," said Mom, "it's getting late. We can keep playing this game OR you can watch a little TV."

"If we watch TV now, can we play the game again tomorrow?" asked Alex.

"Yes," assured Mom.

"Me, too?" asked Alison.

"Oh, sure. I've got more word games for both of you tomorrow."

"Okay," sighed Alex, making his choice. "I'll watch TV now."

Mission accomplished. On this first day of ICPS, Alex had made a decision without a battle and Alison was interested in continuing the game tomorrow. As you can see in the games Marie plays with her children, you can teach word meanings and have fun at the same time.

It's best to play these games before using them in problem-solving situations, especially if your children are very young or don't already know the ICPS vocabulary words. The following examples will get you started on the other ICPS words. Then you can make up more games with picture books, magazines, puppets, dolls, coloring books, and TV shows. Almost any game your child likes to play can be used to practice ICPS words.

Some/All

The words *some* and *all* later help children appreciate that a solution may work some, but not all, of the time. To introduce these words you can use the illustration on page 27, or any picture in a book or magazine. Looking at the picture together, tell your child:

"I'm pointing to ALL the children who are holding something in their hands."

"Now I'm pointing to SOME of the children who are holding something."

Continue demonstrating the words *some* and *all* as you talk about the pictures until you're sure your child understands the concepts. Then you might ask your children questions like these:

"Do ALL the children have a hat on or only SOME of them?"

"Are ALL the children standing or are SOME children standing?"

"Show me ALL the children who are NOT standing."

"Show me SOME children who are NOT standing."

"Now look carefully at the girls. Are ALL the girls wearing a skirt OR are SOME of the girls wearing a skirt?"

"Show me a girl who is NOT wearing a skirt."

Alison's favorite SOME/ALL game is the one she made up while working with her mom in the garden:

"Are ALL the flowers red?" she asked her mom.

"No," laughed Mom, recognizing an ICPS game.

"That's right," Alison agreed. "SOME are pink and SOME are yellow. But ALL the string beans are green, right?"

As Alex came running out to the garden, he heard Alison's game and came up with an idea of his own. "ALL ketchup is red, right?" he shouted proudly.

And so the game continued with Alison, Alex, and their mom making up new ways to practice ICPS vocabulary words.

Before/After

The words *before* and *after* are important concepts needed for consequential thinking; they allow children to realize, "He called me a name AFTER I hit him."

You can teach this concept while working around the house on any two-step process: preparing a bowl of cereal, brushing teeth, making the bed, or even pouring a glass of water:

PARENT: Today's game is about the words BEFORE and AF-TER. Now watch me carefully. I'm turning on the faucet. I turned on the faucet first. Here's what's happening next. Watch. I'm holding the glass under the faucet and putting water in it.

Okay. First, I turned on the faucet. Then I put water in the glass. I turned on the faucet BEFORE I put water in it. I did that first. Did I turn on the faucet (*turn on the faucet*) BEFORE I put water in the glass?

CHILD: (*responds*)

PARENT: Yes, BEFORE. I turned on the faucet. Then what happened next?

CHILD: (*responds*)

PARENT: I put water in the glass. I filled the glass with water AFTER I turned on the faucet. AFTER is what happens

next. Did I put water in the glass AFTER I turned on the faucet?
CHILD: *(responds)*
PARENT: Good!

Now/Later

Now and *later* are words that help children deal with the frustration they feel when they can't have what they want right away. These words help children learn to wait by enabling them to think, "I cannot have that toy NOW. I can play with it LATER." The following dialogue will give you an idea of how you can make sure your children understand this concept.

PARENT: We're playing our ICPS game NOW. What are we doing NOW?
CHILD: *(responds)*
PARENT: Yes, playing our ICPS game. LATER it will be time to go to bed. Is it time to go to bed NOW or LATER?
CHILD: *(responds)*
PARENT: Are we playing our ICPS game BEFORE or AFTER we go to sleep?
CHILD: *(responds)*
PARENT: Yes, BEFORE. Will we go to bed BEFORE or AFTER our ICPS game?
CHILD: *(responds)*
PARENT: Yes, AFTER. We will go to bed LATER.

The games shouldn't feel like workbook exercises—they should feel fun. Look for ways to incorporate these games in your day. You might ask similar questions when you read a bedtime story or while coloring. You can ask your children to color *all* the flowers (or whatever) yellow. You might ask if the wolf knocks on the pigs' door *before* or *after* the pigs build the house. In the morning you can ask if you should cook supper *now* or *later*.

Same/Different

The words *same* and *different* are problem-solving words that will help your children think, "DIFFERENT people can feel DIFFERENT ways about the SAME thing." Also, they'll learn that there are *different* ways to solve the *same* problem.

To begin, show your child two things in the room that are the *same* color.

Show your child two things that are both round.

Show your child two things that are too heavy to lift up.

Then announce, "Okay, today's ICPS game is about the words *SAME* and *DIFFERENT.*"

"I'm going to point to two things and you tell me how they are the SAME." *(Point to two things that are the same color.)*

"Can you guess how these two things are the SAME?"

(Continue with two things that are the same shape, size, weight, etc.)

"Now you point to two things that are the SAME in some way and I'll guess how they are the SAME."

(If you like, increase the number of things that are the same to three things.)

On one particular Saturday afternoon, Alison's friend Tanya was visiting. Tanya was quite shy, and in new or uncomfortable situations, she would often withdraw and refuse to talk at all. Alison's mom noticed that Alison always took the stronger role in their relationship and, in fact, had developed the habit of talking for Tanya.

Marie had thought about Tanya's problem when she was first introduced to ICPS at one of my parent workshops. I mentioned that withdrawn children respond well to this problem-solving approach because it gives them the words and thoughts they need to speak up for themselves. I also mentioned that combining ICPS words with body-movement games is especially useful when working with children who are active, shy, or nonresponsive. Because Alex was so active and Tanya so shy, Marie thought she'd use the following body-movement game to play with the words *same* and *different.*

"I'm raising my hand. Now I'm raising my hand again. I just did the SAME thing. I raised my hand."

"Now I'm going to do something DIFFERENT. I'm going to tap my knee *(tap)*. See, tapping my knee *(keep tapping)* is DIFFERENT from raising my hand *(raise your hand)*."

"Is tapping my knee *(go through the motion)* DIFFERENT from raising my hand *(go through the motion)*?"

(Child responds.)

"Yes, they are DIFFERENT. Tapping my knee is NOT the SAME as raising my hand."

"I'm tapping my knee *(go through the motion)*. Can you do the SAME thing? *(Let child react.)* Good, we're doing the SAME thing."

(A nonresponder can be encouraged by saying: "Let's do it together." Dramatize the act, very emphatically.)

"Can you do something that is NOT the SAME as tapping your knee? *(Let child react.)* Good, you are *(state action)*. That is NOT the SAME as tapping your knee."

"Now, let's have some more fun with the words *SAME* and *DIFFERENT.* Now I'm stamping my foot *(stamp your foot)*. Is stamping my foot the SAME as patting my head? *(Let child respond.)* No, stamping my foot is NOT the SAME as patting my head. It is _____. *(Let child say* different. *It may be necessary to give the choice,* same *or* different, *at least at first.)* Good, they are DIFFERENT."

"Now let's change the game. Now I'm rolling my hands. Can you do something that is NOT the SAME as rolling my hands, something that is DIFFERENT? *(Let child react.)*

Good, you are (state action). That is DIFFERENT from rolling your hands."

(Repeat as long as interest permits, sometimes asking for something that is the same as what you are doing, sometimes asking for something that is different.)

Because Alex, Peter, Alison, and Tanya were all playing the game, Marie let each child take turns being the leader. The leader would do an action and could ask the others to do either the same action or a different one.

When it was Tanya's turn to be the leader, she hung her head and started to walk away, too embarrassed to be the center of attention. Marie quickly drew her back into the game by announcing, "Look, Tanya is walking; let's all do the SAME thing." As the group got up and walked around, Tanya broke into a big smile and changed her action to hopping, giggling as everyone followed her lead.

The next day, Marie knew the children were ready for a somewhat more intricate use of the words same and different. Again, she used an active game to keep Alex's interest.

"Hey Alex, look," began Mom. "I can do two things at the SAME time. I can raise my hand and I can stamp my foot. Can you do two things at the SAME time?"

"Yeah!" yelled Alex wildly. "I can jump and scream at the SAME time."

"Yes, you certainly can," laughed Mom. "Think of two more things you can do at the SAME time. Alison, can you think of two things you can NOT do at the SAME time?"

"Like what?" asked Alison.

"Like, you can't jump and sit at the SAME time."

"Look, Mommy," interrupted Alex. "I'll bet Peter can hop and clap his hands at the SAME time."

"Good!" praised Mom. "Go ahead, Alison, Tell Alex two things he can NOT do at the SAME time."

"You can't do a cartwheel and drink a glass of water at the SAME time."

"Yes, I can," yelled Alex, running to get a glass of water.

"Wait!" called Mom. "Are you teasing me? Can you really do a cartwheel *and* drink water at the SAME time?"

Alex smiled; he knew the answer without his mom having to tell him.

Mom smiled and continued, "Let's play more of our two-things-at-the-SAME-time game. Can I sit in a chair *and* talk on the phone at the SAME time?"

"Yes," chorused Alex and Alison.

"How about this: Alison, can I talk to someone on the phone *and* talk to you at the SAME time?"

"Yes!" yelled Alex.

"Not really," said Alison with a grin.

"And Alex, you answer this: Can I cook dinner *and* read you a story at the SAME time?"

"No," answered Alex.

"So, when can I read you a story—BEFORE or AFTER dinner?"

"AFTER," shouted Alex proudly.

Using ICPS Words in Problem Situations

This mom continued to use ICPS words each day in both special game activities and in her everyday conversations with her children. Repetition of the words in problem situations began to change the way Alex and Alison viewed their problems almost immediately. Instead of turning a negative ear to her refereeing attempts, problem solving became another word game they could play with each other.

After only a week of ICPS word play, Alex and Alison were arguing:

MOM: What's going on?
ALEX: I had it first.
ALISON: I had it first.
MOM: Grabbing is *one* way to get your toy back. What happened AFTER you grabbed?
ALISON: We started fighting.
MOM: Can either of you think of a DIFFERENT way to play so you won't have to fight?
ALISON: I could show him how to play with it.
ALEX: We could play with it together.

Had Mom suggested Alison show Alex how to play with the toy and that they play together, the fighting would probably have continued. The ICPS dialogue let this six- and four-year-old think about how they could solve their own problem. When the solution comes from the children themselves, they tend to think it's a good one.

The word pairs SOME/ALL, SAME/DIFFERENT, and NOW/LATER helped Alex understand his sister on another day. After complaining to his mom, "Alison won't play with me," his mom said, "Alison is doing her homework now. Do you think she can play with you SOME of the time or ALL of the time?"

"ALL of the time," whined Alex.

His mom continued, "Can Alison do her homework AND play with you at the SAME time?"

"I guess not," answered Alex, still unhappy.

"Can you think of something DIFFERENT to do NOW?" asked Mom.

Hesitatingly, Alex replied, "I'll play with my truck."

"Good thinking," said Mom proudly. "Alison can play with you LATER."

Even little Peter was quick to respond to the use of these ICPS words. One evening at dinner, Peter was having a grand time playing with his food and eating with his fingers even though he knew this wasn't allowed. Quieting her impulse to reprimand him, Marie simply said, "We're all eating with our forks and spoons. Peter is eating with his fingers. Is Peter eating the SAME way OR a DIFFERENT way than we are?"

"A DIFFERENT way!" Alex gloated.

"I am NOT," shouted Peter. "The SAME!" And Peter picked up a fork and continued his meal.

What a different and simple way to motivate Peter to eat with his utensils. Whether Peter just forgot the conventional way, or whether he was purposely being funny or disobedient, bringing in the ICPS concepts in this way was more effective than demanding, suggesting, or even explaining.

Finding Daily ICPS Opportunities

Here are more ways you might use ICPS words each day to help your children play with problem-solving concepts. You can also use these daily opportunities to introduce your younger children to word concepts they may still be unsure of. The words *before* and *after*, for example, may still be confusing to some four- and five-year-olds; these games help clarify their meanings.

At Mealtime

"This IS a hamburger. It is NOT an apple. It's also NOT
_____."

"Is this a hamburger OR is it spinach?"

"Are SOME of us eating our beans, or are ALL of us eating our beans?"

"This IS a fork *(point or pick it up)*. This IS a spoon. Is this the SAME thing OR something DIFFERENT?"

"Do you peel your banana BEFORE OR AFTER you eat it?"

"You can eat your cake AFTER you eat SOME of your dinner."

"You can have dessert LATER, *not* NOW."

In the Grocery Store

"This IS a grocery store. It is NOT a toy store. It's also NOT _____."

"This IS a box of cereal AND a container of milk, but NOT chocolate syrup."

"Show me two things that are the SAME."

"We are in the store NOW. What did you do BEFORE we came to the store?"

"Can we be in the store AND at home at the SAME time?"

Watching TV

"That man IS eating AND talking, but he is NOT laughing. He is also NOT _____."

"Do we like the SAME TV shows OR DIFFERENT TV shows?"

"Do we watch TV BEFORE OR AFTER we do homework?"

In the Car

"This IS a car. It is NOT a lollipop. It is also NOT a _____."

"We're riding AND talking, but NOT walking. What else are we not doing? We are NOT _____."

"Can we ride AND talk at the SAME time?"

"Can we ride AND walk at the SAME time?"

"What do we do right AFTER we get into the car? Fasten our _____ (seat belts)."

While Dressing

"Are you putting on pants OR are you putting on a dress?"

"Bring me your socks AND your shoes AND your red shirt, but NOT your blue shirt."

"Are your shirt AND your pants the SAME color OR are they a DIFFERENT color?"

"Did you put your shoes on BEFORE OR AFTER you put on your socks?"

"Do you get dressed BEFORE OR AFTER you get out of bed?"

"Can you lie in bed AND get dressed at the SAME time?"

Anytime

"Today IS Tuesday. *(Child responds.)* No? It is NOT Tuesday. Oh, it IS (Saturday)."

"It IS sunny outside. It is NOT rainy. It is also NOT _____."

"Do you put your toys away BEFORE OR AFTER you play with them?"

"SOME apples are red. SOME apples are green. Are ALL apples red?"

"Are ALL the chairs in this room green?"

"Are SOME of the chairs in this room green?"

"Are ALL dogs white OR are SOME dogs white?"

"What color are people's eyes? Do ALL people have blue eyes? No, SOME people have blue eyes. SOME people have _____ eyes."

Responding to Behavior

When your children are interacting with other children, ask them: "IS what you're doing (*grabbing toys, sharing, etc.*) a good idea OR NOT a good idea?" (*Ask this question often when your child is doing positive things as well as negative things.)*

When your children nag you for attention, tell them: "I can NOT (read, play, whatever) with you NOW. Maybe I can spend time with you LATER. Can you think of something DIFFERENT to do NOW?"

You can also draw upon the phrase "two things at the *same time*" in these kinds of situations. For example, you can ask, "Can I talk to you AND talk on the phone at the SAME time?" After your child responds, you can follow with, "Can you think of something DIFFERENT to do NOW?"

When your children have to make a choice, tell them: "You can have candy OR pie, but NOT candy AND pie." Or: "You can play with SOME of the toys, but NOT ALL of the toys."

You may wish to make a list of the ICPS word pairs you have used with your child thus far and, as a reminder, stick it up on your refrigerator or some other convenient place:

IS/IS NOT	BEFORE/AFTER
AND/OR	NOW/LATER
SOME/ALL	SAME/DIFFERENT

Using ICPS words during your daily routine will teach your children to associate them with fun, and even at this early stage in ICPS dialoguing your children can begin to think in problem-solving ways.

3

◆ • ◆

Understanding Feelings

One spring afternoon, four-year-old Alex had a problem and a common, but insensitive, solution. He wanted to ride his bike, but his sister Alison was riding it. Without warning, Alex pushed Alison off the bike, jumped on it himself, and rode away. This is certainly a typical scene on any playground, and many child-development experts think it happens because young children are unable to consider how their actions make others feel. My research has found this isn't so. Even preschool children can learn to tune into feelings and use this information to solve their social problems.

When children don't learn to consider others' feelings, they can carry this problem-solving handicap into their adult lives. Consider thirty-year-old Larry, for example. At the real estate office where he works, Larry is known for being selfish and insensitive. He accepts clients he knows he should refer to other agents; he makes appointments at inappropriate hours; and he arranges meetings without considering the schedules of his co-workers and clients. People who work with Larry get angry and frustrated because he doesn't stop to think how his actions make others feel.

In truth, many people like Larry aren't really selfish or insensitive; they've just never learned to consider other people's feelings when they make decisions. Unfortunately, because they lack this component of the problem-solving equation, they have few friends and frequently face career obstacles. Children, too, often lose friends and face daily obstacles because they act without considering how their actions make others feel.

The second step in ICPS problem solving helps children develop the habit of thinking about feelings as they solve their daily problems. A child with Alex's problem will learn to stop and think: "If I don't get my bike back, I'll be mad, but if I push Alison off the bike, she'll be mad." This is a first step away from the "Larry" track and toward the habit of looking for lots of solutions, including ones that are fair and considerate of everyone's needs—a skill children can bring with them into their teen and adult lives.

When Mom was sure Alex and Alison had used the ICPS problem-solving words presented in the last chapter often enough to recognize them readily and associate them with their play games, she began adding feeling words and questions to her ICPS dialogues. The feeling words most often involved in problem solving (and the focus of ICPS games) are *happy, sad, angry, proud,* and *frustrated.*

Reading Pictures

One evening, while Alison was at a school meeting with her dad, Mom called Alex to join her in the kitchen. (Two-year-old Peter, of course, tagged along.) While she poured them both some juice, Mom explained how they could use the ICPS vocabulary words they talked about last week to play a new game about feelings. Mom showed Alex the illustrations on page 43. (You can use these drawings or any pictures of your own.) Using the vocabulary words *is* and *not*, she asked Alex to identify the emotions of the children in the pictures.

Pointing to the smiling boy, Mom said, "This boy IS smiling. Do you think he is HAPPY?"

"Yeah," said Alex, only barely interested.

Pointing to the girl who is crying, she said, "This girl is NOT smiling. Do you think she is HAPPY?"

"No," said Alex. "She's crying."

"No," echoed Peter.

"How do you think she feels?"

"I don't know."

Trying to remain patient and pleasant despite Alex's negative answers, Mom asked, "HAPPY?" as she made a happy face. "Or SAD?" as she dramatically made a sad face.

Realizing Alex needed to be more actively involved in the game, Mom continued, "Now you point to the picture of the child who IS HAPPY."

Alex pointed to the happy child.

"Good. Now point to the picture of the child who is NOT happy."

Alex again pointed to the picture of the happy child and fell on the floor laughing at his own silly response. Mom knew he was just teasing her.

Some children will occasionally give silly, irrelevant, or opposite answers. Others may laugh hysterically or make faces. If this happens when you use ICPS dialogues with your children, follow this mother's example and continue with the lesson with a positive attitude. Anger and scoldings tend to encourage more of this kind of behavior. Silly behavior often diminishes as children become more comfortable with the concepts of the program. When your "silly" children do respond normally, be sure to praise their efforts.

Alex, Peter, and their mom kept playing the game, switching back and forth between pointing to a child smiling and not smiling, crying and not crying, happy and not happy, sad and not sad. When Alex or Peter would answer incorrectly (either purposely or not), Mom would simply repeat (while using

dramatic facial expressions) that a smiling child probably feels happy and a crying child probably feels sad and then ask the question again.

Mom and Alex were still playing when Alison and her dad arrived home. When Alison asked what the pictures were for, Alex suddenly became an enthusiastic expert on ICPS feeling words.

"You have to point to one of the pictures," Alex explained, "and say if the boy or girl is HAPPY or SAD. Like this." *(Pointing to the girl)* "She's SAD."

"How can you tell?" asked Alex's dad.

"Because she's crying," answered Alex as Peter mimicked a sad expression.

"I can do that," said Alison. "Watch." *(Pointing to the boy)* "HAPPY." *(Pointing to the girl)* "SAD. See, it's easy."

"Maaa!" Alex began to cry as he hit Alison. He wanted her to be more excited about this new game.

"Alison," interrupted Mom, "Alex and Peter like pointing to the faces. Let's see if you can remember how to use two of our vocabulary words with the pictures."

"What do you mean?" Alison asked.

"Do this boy and this girl" *(pointing to the sad face and the happy face pictures)* "have the SAME feelings, or do they have DIFFERENT feelings?"

"DIF-FER-ENT," answered Alison, having fun with the word.

"Yes," Mom said. "They have DIFFERENT feelings. They do NOT feel the SAME way. That was good. Do you think that sometimes you and Alex feel DIFFERENT ways about the SAME thing?"

"Yes," said Alison.

"Now let's get ready for bed," said Dad, "and you guys can play more word games tomorrow."

In future ICPS dialogues Mom will often repeat this emphasis on *same* and *different* to help her children see that different people might feel different ways about the same thing.

Reading Other People's Feelings

The next day after dinner Mom continued the game about feelings with an emphasis on the three ways we can tell how other people feel.

"Let's talk about our eyes and ears," Mom said. "Show me your eyes." Mom pointed to her own eyes as Peter, Alex, and Alison pointed to theirs. "I can see with my eyes. What do you do with your eyes?" Mom asked Alex.

"I see with my eyes too!" said Alex.

"Me too!" said Peter.

"Now show me your ears." Mom pointed to her own ears as Peter, Alex, and Alison pointed to theirs. "Can we see with our ears?" Mom asked Alison.

"No!" yelled Alison. "We hear with our ears."

"You're right," agreed Mom. "What about our eyes?" she kidded. "Can we hear with our eyes?"

"Mommy!" giggled Alex.

"We can NOT hear with our eyes. You're silly," laughed Alison.

"You're all very smart," said Mom. "You know we see with our eyes and we hear with our ears. Okay, now let's see how clever you really are." Mom covered her face with a sheet of paper and laughed very dramatically. "Am I HAPPY or am I SAD?"

"You're HAPPY," yelled Alex and Alison together.

"HAPPY," agreed Peter.

"How can you tell I'm HAPPY?"

"Because you're laughing," said Alison.

"How can you tell I'm laughing? Did you see me with your eyes?"

"No," answered Alex.

"Did you hear me with your ears?"

"Yes," answered Alison.

"Yes, you heard me with your ears. Let's try it again."

Mom repeated the game by hiding her face and crying. Again, Alex and Alison guessed that she was sad because they could hear her cry with their ears.

"Now we have two ways to find out how someone feels. One way you can tell I'm HAPPY is to see me with your eyes." Mom pointed to her eyes. "Another way is to hear with your ears." And she pointed to her ears.

"There is another way you can tell how a person feels," continued Mom. Keeping a straight, unemotional face, she said, "Can you tell how I feel?"

"You're mad," guessed Alex.

Mom shook her head.

"You're thinking," guessed Alison.

Mom shook her head. "How could you find out how I feel?"

"How?" asked Alison.

"You can *ask* people how they feel. Ask me how I feel."

"I want to!" yelled Alex, wanting to beat his sister to the question. "How do you feel?" he asked.

"I feel HAPPY. How do you feel?"

"I feel happy," said Alison.

"I feel tired," said Alex.

"How did I find out how you feel?"

"You asked us," chorused Alex and Alison as Peter watched and giggled.

"Yes, I did because that's a good way to find out how people feel."

This exercise helps children consider how other people feel. This skill will give your children more options when they try to solve problems at home, at school, or anywhere. They'll learn how to judge how someone feels about their actions and decisions.

While playing these games, Marie started to think about how she usually determines how her children are feeling. She tried to think of a time when she found out how Alison was feeling by *seeing* what she was doing. How often, she wondered, had she actually asked her children how they were feeling? After thinking about this, Marie discovered that most often she only knows when she hears them say, "I'm so happy," or, "I'm scared." Now Marie realized that she could learn more about her children's feelings by using ICPS skills herself.

Using the same kind of activities that began this exploration of feelings, you can move the focus to the word *angry* by asking your children to look at the illustration on page 47. Repeat the eyes and ears activity by creating a dialogue that asks:

"Does this boy look HAPPY?" "How can you tell?"

"Can you hear with your ears?" "Can you see with your eyes?"

"If you could ask him, 'How do you feel?' Do you think he would say he is ANGRY?"

"Can you see that with your eyes?"

"How do you think an ANGRY person sounds?"

"Is this boy feeling the SAME or DIFFERENT than this boy (on page 43), who is smiling?"

"What do you think might be making this boy ANGRY?"

"What things make *you* ANGRY?"

Children feel at ease talking about things that make them feel angry because, in game form, they can feel safe talking about uncomfortable emotions.

As Marie helped her children think about their own and

others' feelings, she also began to think about *her* feelings and how what *she* does affects others, including her children.

During this word play with emotions, you might ask yourself a few ICPS questions: What does your child do or say that makes you feel happy? Sad? Angry? Now turn this around: What do *you* do or say that might make your child feel happy? Sad? Angry? The answers to these simple questions will give you some insight into how much you consider others' feelings in your own life.

After school one day, Alison, her friend Tanya, and Marie were waiting in the school gym for the start of their soccer game. Marie had ended her feeling games with Alex and Peter with the words *happy, sad,* and *angry* because the emotions of frustration and pride are complex and difficult for very young children to grasp. But she thought she'd see if Alison and Tanya could go further with the new ICPS words *frustrated* and *proud.*

"Do you ever feel FRUSTRATED when you try to make a soccer goal but can't?" Marie asked Alison.

"What's FRUSTRATED?"

"FRUSTRATED is when things do not go the way you want them to, or when you want something you can not have, you may feel FRUSTRATED. Like how you feel when you want to talk to someone and the person is busy?"

"Angry," said Alison.

"ANGRY, and . . . what's our big new word?" asked Marie.

"FRUSTRATED."

"Good. How about you, Tanya? How do you feel when you want to watch TV but your mother says it's time for bed?"

As Tanya looked away from Marie, Alison yelled, "FRUS-TRATED!"

"Did you feel FRUSTRATED, Tanya?"

Tanya nodded her head yes.

"Good, Tanya. You can also feel FRUSTRATED when you try to do something and you can't. Like maybe you try to skate but you keep falling down. Or you might feel FRUSTRATED if you can't get your shoelace tied. Has anything like this ever happened to you, Alison?"

"Yeah, like reading," said Alison quickly. "I keep trying to read my books by myself, but I can't."

"That's a good example," praised Marie. "That feeling you get when you try to read a story but can't figure out all the words is called FRUSTRATION. What about you, Tanya, what makes you feel FRUSTRATED?"

When Tanya stared blankly at Marie, Alison jumped in to help. "Like when you were standing on your head and kept falling down. Is that FRUSTRATED?"

Then Marie asked, "Tanya, did you feel FRUSTRATED when you couldn't stand on your head?"

Tanya nodded yes.

"Well," said Marie, "I know you can stand on your head now. That feeling you had when you finally learned how to do it is called PROUD. I cooked a very delicious dinner last night and I felt PROUD. A girl I know ran a race and won it; she felt PROUD. Alison, what makes you feel PROUD?"

"I don't know."

"Well, how do you feel when you get a star on your school paper? That feeling is called PROUD."

"How about when I set the table without you telling me to?" asked Alison.

"Yes, that's a good example; you probably do feel PROUD when you do that. How about you, Tanya, what makes you feel PROUD?"

When Tanya didn't answer, Marie motioned to Alison not to answer for her, and then asked, "Tanya, Alison told me that you drew a picture of your house that was so pretty the teacher hung it on the wall in your classroom. Did you feel PROUD when she did that?"

Tanya nodded her head.

"Good," said Marie, knowing it would take more time before Tanya felt sure enough of these ICPS games to join in verbally.

"Well, girls, how about making me feel PROUD of you by playing your best in this game today. Okay?"

"Okay, Mom," laughed Alison.

Tanya just smiled.

If your children are shy like Tanya, make it easy for them to participate in ICPS games and dialogues. Ask simple questions so they can give one-word responses or shake or nod their head. For example, "When you learned to skate, did you feel PROUD or ANGRY?" If you continually praise any level of participation and give them lots of opportunities to respond, you'll soon see that ICPS equips them with the thinking processes they need to feel more secure about voicing their needs and feelings.

As Marie watched Alison and Tanya play their soccer game, she started to think more about the feelings of pride and frustration. You might do the same thing by asking yourself these kinds of questions:

"When was a time when my child was PROUD of me? How could I tell?"

"When was the last time I felt PROUD of my child?"

"When was a time I felt FRUSTRATED about something?"

"Was there ever a time my children were FRUSTRATED with me?"

As you continue to teach feeling words to your children, your answers to these questions will sensitize you to your own and your child's point of view. You may come to realize that *all* of you may *not* see things the *same* way *all* the time.

Talking About Feelings

With just a bit of alteration, many of the activities your children already enjoy can be used to practice thinking and talking about feelings.

Story Time

As you read through your child's storybooks, stop at various points in the story and ask your child to guess how one of the book's characters feels. Ask how we can tell. Whatever the story line, spend time talking about each character's feelings.

Story time is also a good opportunity to make up stories about people and how they feel. Encourage your child to add details to the story that explain why the character feels sad and what he or she might do to feel happy. Talk about how the hero feels when he or she saves the day. Ask your children if they have ever had feelings like the character in the book.

Drawing

Because coloring was one of Alex's favorite activities, Marie decided to begin reinforcing the idea of thinking about others' feelings by drawing pictures. She asked Alex to draw a picture of a happy face. Marie drew one also. Then she asked Alex to draw another face, but this time a sad one.

"How can you tell that one face is HAPPY and the other face is SAD?" Marie asked.

"Because one IS smiling, and one is NOT," reasoned Alex. Marie reinforced Alex's observation by asking, "And how can you tell she's smiling? You can see with your _____ (*pointing to her eyes*)."

Alex quickly jumped in with, *"Eyes!"*

Pointing to the picture, Marie, slightly smiling, quipped, "Can you ask her?"

Alex laughed. "No, silly. You can't ask a picture." Alex and his mom continued the drawing game by drawing happy and sad animals, flowers, pumpkins, and dolls.

If you choose this drawing game, you might also help your child look through coloring books for happy, sad, angry, proud, or frustrated faces and then color those you find.

Puppet Play

Puppet play is a wonderful way to reinforce ICPS concepts. (If you don't have any puppets, dolls, stuffed animals, paper bags with crayoned faces, or even socks can be used in the same way.) Make up little stories that demonstrate happy and sad situations. You might also add characters who help other characters feel better. Changing your voice in the character of the puppet, a simple puppet play might sound like this:

DOG PUPPET: I think I'm going to cry.

CAT PUPPET: Why? What's the matter?

DOG PUPPET: All the other dogs ran outside to play and they didn't ask me to come along.

CAT PUPPET: (*to child*) How do you think the dog feels now?

After he or she answers, the cat responds, "Yes, SAD. What else makes *you* feel SAD?"

Now let your children pick up these puppet friends often to help them express their feelings and create their own stories about their own and others' feelings.

Feeling Word Games

Feeling word games can be used to reinforce this lesson even when you're driving the car, washing the dishes, or taking care of siblings. For example, while you're seated around the dinner table, tell your children:

"I'm going to tell you three things that make me feel HAPPY. Listen carefully because you have to remember them: one, eating ice cream; two, wearing my jewelry; and three, seeing you smile. Who can remember my three things?

"Now I'm going to add a fourth thing. Ready: one, eating ice cream; two, wearing my jewelry; three, seeing you smile; and four, when you do *not* scream. Can you remember my four things?"

Add a fifth and sixth and so on until your children can no longer remember the list. Then let your children make up their own lists and see if you can remember. You can play this game with any of the feeling words.

It's fun to think of things that affect the feelings of other people. Thinking about their own and others' feelings will later open up problem-solving options that are not available to children who think only of their own needs at the moment.

TV Games

TV time offers many opportunities for talking about feelings. With whatever shows your children watch, you can use dialogues like the following to encourage your children to use the ICPS thinking skills they've learned so far.

"Look, that boy is smiling." "How does he feel?" "How can you tell he is HAPPY?" "Can you see him laughing with your eyes?" "Can you hear him with your ears?" "Can you ask him?"

"Why is (*name of character*) ANGRY? What happened that made him/her feel that way?"

"Look, that girl is crying. What can she do to feel HAPPY again?"

"My-Own" Games

In my experience with families who use ICPS, I've found that once children grasp the concept of a given emotion, they're often quick to make up their own games. This is a good sign that the children understand and enjoy the games, and it also gives the ICPS program the flexibility that makes it unique in each home.

Marie was delighted by a game Alex created himself. As Alex smiled, laughed, and jumped around, he told his mom that he was pretending to be an actor on TV who was happy. When Marie asked him what was making him feel happy, Alex quickly decided it was the actor's birthday. Then Alex pretended to be a sad actor. Again Marie asked why the actor was sad. "Because," said Alex, "he has no friends to play with."

This unique game, enacting many happy and sad circumstances, encouraged Alex to think about what makes other people feel happy or sad. Alex liked this game best of all (probably because he invented it) and continued to play it with other emotions in later lessons. If your children think of activities that focus on feelings, don't hesitate to go along with their games.

Using ICPS in Problem Situations

The first opportunity to test the usefulness of these activities came when Alex started to draw on the wall. Before ICPS, Marie would have said something like, "Alex, don't write on the walls because it makes a mess and it's hard to get off! I'll help you find something else to write on, but don't do this again. Do you understand?" Alex would have dutifully replied, "Yes, Mommy," and probably would have marked up the walls again a week later. Although Marie tried to use parenting approaches she had read about, like giving reasons why the action was wrong and offering positive alternatives, she was still doing the thinking for Alex, and so her past disciplinary responses were quite different from an ICPS response. Realizing now that Alex hadn't really listened to those scoldings, Marie tried an ICPS dialogue something like this:

MOM: When you do something I do NOT want you to do, how do you think I feel?

ALEX: Mad.

MOM: Do you and I feel the SAME way OR a DIFFERENT way about this?

ALEX: A different way.

MOM: Do you know why I do NOT want you to write on the walls?

ALEX: 'Cause you can't get it off.

MOM: And why else?

ALEX: It's messy.

MOM: Can you think of a DIFFERENT place to write so you won't make a mess and I will NOT feel ANGRY?

ALEX: (*after a moment*) On paper.

MOM: Good thinking.

Using the words *not, same, different,* and *or,* which Alex learned in earlier games, Alex's mother helped him think about why she didn't want him to draw on the walls and where else he could draw. This kind of dialogue allows Alex to become engaged in *how* he can change his behavior rather than merely respond to directions *to* change his behavior.

Later that same day Marie walked into Alison's room and found her toys, pillows, and clothes flung all over. Feeling somewhat exasperated, Marie could not hold back her anger, but still clung to the ICPS way of dealing with the situation.

"Alison!" cried Mom. "How do you think I feel when I see your room looking like this?"

Recognizing an ICPS dialogue, Alison sheepishly grinned and guessed, "Sad?"

"No, I'm NOT sad. Can you think of a way to find out how I feel?"

"I could ask you, right?"

"Okay," said Mom. "Go ahead and ask me."

"How do you feel, Mom?"

"I feel very angry and I feel FRUSTRATED, too. Do you remember what FRUSTRATED means?"

"Yeah, it's like when I try to win the game but don't?"

"Exactly. Well, I've asked you over and over to keep this room clean but you don't, so how do you think I feel?"

"FRUSTRATED," answered Alison.

Maybe you have felt like this but your children didn't understand your reaction because they didn't know the meaning of, or think much about, the word *frustrated.*

This mom continued, "Can you think of a DIFFERENT place to put your clothes so I won't feel this way?"

"Yes," said Alison. "I could put them in my closet and I can find a DIFFERENT place to put my toys too."

"Okay, you decide where to hang your clothes and where to put your toys. This will make me very PROUD of you."

"Okay, Mom."

In this dialogue, Alison's mom helped her think about how her messy room affected other people. Also, while she did not give Alison a choice about whether or not to clean her room, she did allow her the choice about *how* to clean her room.

Some parents have mentioned to me that they're afraid ICPS will cause them to lose control over their children or forfeit their right to discipline. As the above example shows, this needn't be a concern. Discipline whose only purpose is to control children's behavior or to teach them what to do by telling them how to do it, can make them feel helpless and lower their sense of self-esteem. But with ICPS, discipline means helping children think about behavior patterns that are adaptive; it means giving them a sense of control over their lives. In that sense, ICPS problem solving *is* discipline.

This is not to say that you should never get angry with your children while using ICPS. That would be unnatural. Anger is itself a problem children must learn to cope with. They can learn to do that if they are encouraged to think about anger as a social problem—and if anger and emotional outbursts are not the most common forms of dealing with confrontation in the child's home. Alison's messy room made her mom feel very angry, but she didn't lose control over her daughter or forfeit her right to discipline either.

In developing the ICPS program for you and your children, I recognized the need not only to help you teach your children how to think and how to see your point of view, but also to help you become more sensitive to your children's points of view. When this happens you'll see that discipline takes on a new and more positive focus.

ICPS Mini-Dialogues: Problem Situations

Compare how the parents below talked to their children before ICPS and how they learned to use the ICPS concepts we've covered so far.

When Your Child Interrupts You

Before ICPS, Tim's mother would typically say, "You're making me really angry! You know I can't talk to you while I'm on the phone. Leave me alone!" After playing with ICPS words, his mother now says, "Can I talk to you AND to my friend at the SAME time?" She may also add, "How do you think I feel when you interrupt me when I'm on the phone?" If needed, she follows with, "How do you think my friend feels when I have to stop and talk to you?" Most often Tim is willing to wait for his mother's attention when she reminds him, "I know you have something you want to tell me. I will listen to you AFTER I finish talking to my friend. Can you think of something DIFFERENT to do now that will make us both feel happy?"

This use of ICPS words helps children think about how interrupting affects your feelings and your friend's feelings. It also creates a very different mood than if you were to ignore your children or verbally chase them away. One ICPS mother told me that her six-year-old interrupted her when she was trying to talk to the doctor, and she turned to him and simply said, "Can I talk to you AND to the doctor at the SAME time?" With a proud smile, her son replied, "No, and I can think of something DIFFERENT to do."

When Your Child Is Not Paying Attention

One non-ICPS way to handle a child who does not pay attention is to say in an angry tone, "You know I can't stand it when you don't listen to me. Look at me and pay attention when I talk to you!" Another is to talk about your feelings: "I feel

ANGRY when you don't listen to me." Although this is not as threatening as the first response, because you are telling your child how you feel, you're still doing the thinking for the child.

An ICPS parent asks the child to *think* about how the parent feels: "If you do NOT listen when I talk to you, how do you think I feel? What can you do so I will NOT feel that way?"

When Your Child Wants Something at an Inconvenient Time

Four-year-old Sean wanted his mom to read him a story. When his mom told him she was busy helping his sister with her homework, Sean continued to whine, "But I want you to read to me *now!*" Before ICPS this mom would have said, "You have to learn to wait. You can't always have everything the minute you want it. If you act like that I won't read to you at all. You're not being fair to your sister."

After having played games with the ICPS words *all* and *some,* and games with the feeling words, Sean's mom now turned to her son and said, "How might your sister feel if I read to you ALL of the time and did NOT help her SOME of the time?" Sean recognized the words of his ICPS games and simply smiled. He understood.

Who's doing the thinking now?

◆　　◆　　◆

When Marie reached this point in the ICPS program, she thought back to a time before she began using ICPS when she waged a daily battle trying to keep Alex from tormenting his younger brother, Peter. Whenever Marie wasn't looking, Alex would do something to make his brother cry. One day she walked into the room just in time to catch Alex in the act of grabbing Peter's teddy bear away from him. Her response followed its usual format:

"What's going on here?" Marie shouted.

Alex shrugged, giving her that "I don't know and I don't care" look.

"If you can't play nice with Peter, then stay away from him! He doesn't like it when you take away his toys."

Without a word, Alex ran to his room. Marie just shook her head, wondering how she was ever going to get Alex to treat his brother more kindly.

After about two weeks of playing with ICPS vocabulary and feeling words, Marie once again heard Peter's scream from the next room and ran in to find Alex pulling his bear away from him. This time she tried an ICPS dialogue:

"How do you think Peter feels when you grab his bear like that?"

"Mad," replied Alex.

Mom then asked, "And what happens when you do that?"

"He screams."

"And how does that make *you* feel?" continued Mom.

"Sad."

"Can you think of something DIFFERENT to do so he won't feel mad and you won't feel SAD when he screams?" his mom asked.

Alex gave Peter back his toy. He was not yet ready to feel genuine empathy, and he still was not able to figure out how to relate to Peter in more positive ways. But for now Marie was happy to see that he was willing to solve the problem after considering how Peter might feel. She knew this was an important first step.

4

More ICPSing

Marie soon grew into the habit of asking questions like:

"Do ALL the children at this table want pancakes, OR do SOME want cereal?"

"Should I eat this apple BEFORE or AFTER I wash it?"

"Do you and your sister feel the SAME way about this problem OR do you feel a DIFFERENT way?"

It wasn't long before Marie noticed that her children were even using ICPS words among themselves. When Alison jumped into the front seat of the family car, Alex yelled, "You can't sit in the front ALL the time—just SOME."

"The way he emphasized the words *some* and *all*," said Marie, "I knew he was consciously using those ICPS words to make his point more valid. Alison still wouldn't move, but I was impressed with the way he tried."

When Alison wouldn't accept Alex's logical reason for getting out of the front seat, he reverted to his usual behavior: hitting and crying. Soon after this happened, Marie asked me why, after using ICPS words for several weeks, Alex still couldn't solve his problems more effectively. I assured her that she shouldn't expect her children to do this just yet. The ICPS vocabulary words are practiced as part of the *pre–problem-solving activities* so that later they can be incorporated into full ICPS dialogues. The stronger this vocabulary base, the easier and more effectively children progress to actually using them when the time comes to solve problems.

Before moving to actual problem-solving dialogues, you have one more group of word concepts to introduce to your children: GOOD TIME/NOT A GOOD TIME, IF/THEN, MIGHT/MAYBE, WHY/BECAUSE, FAIR/NOT FAIR. This group of words represents another step forward in thinking skills. They will help your children prepare to accept limitations they can't change: "This is NOT A GOOD TIME for me to read you a story." They'll avoid the frustration so often associated with personal conflicts, as one child might say to another: "IF you sit in the front seat on the way to the store, THEN I sit there on the way home. Okay?" They'll have the words they need to explain themselves: "I can't share my candy BECAUSE it's all gone." And they'll have more words that are important precursors to later consequential thinking: "IF I grab his toy, THEN he MIGHT grab it back." "He hit me BECAUSE . . ." These words plus the earlier ones *before* and *after* can help children think, "He hit me AFTER I hit him."

As these word pairs are introduced to Alison, Alex, and Tanya, you'll notice that the ICPS words and emotions practiced in Chapters Two and Three continue to be an important part of ICPS talk. Together these concepts provide a dynamic set of tools that later help children recognize and foresee the sequence of events in interpersonal relations. The ICPS mini-dialogues in this chapter will include new ICPS word concepts and combine the use of all previously used ICPS vocabulary words.

Team Work

Each day Tanya left Alison's house and ran home to tell her mother more about the word games Alison and her mom liked to play. "Tanya is quite shy," says her mom, Karena. "So I was surprised to hear her tell stories about games she played and questions she answered in front of Alison's mother." After a few weeks of hearing about these games, Karena called Marie to find out more about what Tanya called ICPSing.

Marie invited Karena over to her house to show her the materials I had distributed at the ICPS workshop. When Marie explained the significant advantages of this program for shy children, Karena was very eager to make copies of the material and work with Tanya at her house also. Thus, an ICPS parent team was created.

Although ICPS has proven very successful in individual homes and with a single child, working through ICPS as a team has some advantages you might want to consider. As a parent team, Maria and Karena and their husbands built their own little support group; they shared their successes and setbacks; they talked about their problems, concerns, and triumphs, and they gave each other encouragement to continue. Children (especially those who are the only child) also benefit from family teams. They learn the skills in a gamelike situation with other children. They have more opportunities for practicing these new skills with friends who are familiar with the ICPS concepts and respond positively to them.

Good Time/Not a Good Time

The word phrases GOOD TIME/NOT A GOOD TIME help children learn that timing is an important ingredient in successful problem solving. Karena will include this concept in her games with Tanya with the help of two puppets—Ollie and Tippy.

Withdrawn or shy children are especially fond of puppets because they can let the puppets say things they're too inhibited to say themselves. Puppets are also useful for teaching all children these final pre-ICPS concepts because puppet play demonstrates how the words can be used in problem situations.

If you choose, you can substitute stuffed animals, dolls, or even two socks of different colors. You can use a script like the following, which Karena used to play the GOOD TIME/NOT A GOOD TIME game with Tanya, or you can ad lib. Either way, the goal is to show your children two "people" who are learning that knowing when to time requests is one way to avoid conflicts and frustration.

Karena's scene with the two puppets Ollie and Tippy (using two different voices) went something like this:

OLLIE: *(to Tanya)* Hi, Tanya. How are you today? I saw—
TIPPY: *(interrupting)* Hi, Ollie. Want to play with me?
OLLIE: Tippy, can I talk to you AND to Tanya at the SAME time?
TIPPY: No.
OLLIE: How do you think I feel when you interrupt me?
TIPPY: ANGRY.
OLLIE: Is this a GOOD TIME or NOT A GOOD TIME to talk to me?
TIPPY: NOT A GOOD TIME.
OLLIE: How do you think my friend feels when I am talking to her and I have to stop and talk to you?
TIPPY: ANGRY AND FRUSTRATED.
OLLIE: I know you have something you want to tell me. You can tell me AFTER I finish talking to my friend. Just wait now.

OLLIE: *(to Tanya)* Let's have lunch soon. I like hamburgers AND french fries. What do you like to eat?

TANYA: I like cheese sandwiches.

OLLIE: Oh, I like that too. What else do you like to eat?

TANYA: I like tuna fish.

OLLIE: Really. I like that SOME of the time, NOT ALL of the time.

OLLIE: *(turning to Tippy)* Okay, Tippy. I'm very PROUD of you. You waited very well. Now I can listen to what you want to tell me.

TIPPY: Will you play with me NOW?

OLLIE: Yes, I will. Is this a GOOD TIME to ask me?

TIPPY: Yes.

OLLIE: Was it a GOOD TIME to ask me to play BEFORE I finished talking to my friend?

TIPPY: No. AFTER.

OLLIE: Good. I am NOT talking to my friend NOW.

When Karena finished this puppet scene, she asked Tanya, "Ollie couldn't talk to you and Tippy at the SAME time, could he? Sometimes we all have to wait for a GOOD TIME to get what we want."

"Let's do that again, please," begged Tanya.

"All right, Tanya," said her mom. "Let's pretend Ollie wants to read this book, and Tippy wants to play."

OLLIE: *(looks busy reading a book)*

TIPPY: Ollie, will you play with me?

OLLIE: No, Tippy. I'm busy NOW.

TIPPY: *(with head down, turns away sadly)*

OLLIE: *(Continues reading his book. Then stops and closes the book)* Okay, I'm finished reading.

TIPPY: Hi, Ollie. Can you play with me NOW?

OLLIE: Yes. I'm NOT busy NOW.

After this little scene between Ollie and Tippy, this mom asked her daughter, "When did Tippy pick a better time to ask Ollie to read a story, BEFORE Ollie was finished reading his book OR AFTER he was finished reading his book?"

"After," said Tanya.

"Good thinking. Can you think of a time when someone asked you to do something when you were busy doing something?"

"Yep!" said Tanya. "Alison wanted to ride bikes, but I was coloring a picture."

"So what happened?"

"Alison went home ANGRY."

"Did she ask you to ride bikes at a GOOD TIME or NOT A GOOD TIME?"

"NOT A GOOD TIME," replied Tanya excitedly. "Mom, can I be Ollie now and you be Tippy?"

This is how Tanya and her mom began using ICPS in their house. Tanya knew all the earlier ICPS words from her games with Alison's mom; now she was delighted to play with her own mom.

ICPS Mini-Dialogues: Problem Situations

I'll bet you certainly can think of times when your children have asked you to do something when you were busy doing something else. After your puppet play with GOOD TIME/ NOT A GOOD TIME, it's easy to use these words in your daily conversations.

When Your Child Interrupts You

"Can I talk to you AND to my friend at the same time?"

"If you talk to me while I'm talking to someone else, how do you think I feel? (If needed: HAPPY or FRUSTRATED?)"

"If I'm talking to someone, is that a GOOD TIME or NOT A GOOD TIME to try to talk to me?"

"When IS a good time?"

"Can you think of something DIFFERENT to do until I can talk to you?"

When Your Child Wants to Play at an Inconvenient Time

"You want to ride your bike NOW, but we're about to have dinner."

"Can you ride your bike AND eat dinner at the SAME time?"

"Is this a GOOD TIME or NOT A GOOD TIME to ride your bike?"

"When IS a good time?"

"Can you think of something DIFFERENT to do NOW?"

When Your Child Wants Your Attention When You're Busy

"I can't talk to you NOW; I'm helping Jeffrey do his homework."

"Can I talk to you AND help Jeffrey at the SAME time?"

"Is this a GOOD TIME or NOT A GOOD TIME to talk to me?"

"When IS a good time?"

"Can you think of something DIFFERENT to do NOW?"

The following Saturday morning, Tanya was up, dressed, and running out the door at nine o'clock. With her puppets in hand, she was off to show her new game to Alison and Alex.

"Tanya was so excited," remembers Alison's mom. "I had introduced the phrases GOOD TIME/NOT A GOOD TIME to Alison and Alex by talking about circumstances we've experienced when we all chose *not a good time* to ask for something. So my kids were familiar with the words and their use. But Tanya's idea of using puppets to act out GOOD TIME/ NOT A GOOD TIME scenarios was a good way to review. It was probably the first time I saw Tanya take charge when she was with my kids."

Already, ICPS was helping Tanya find the words to speak up.

If/Then

Each of these word games prepares your children to meet the ultimate goal of ICPS: effectively solving their own people-problems. The word pair IF/THEN is a first step toward the kind of consequential thinking they need to do this successfully.

Daily Use: Nonproblem Situations

You can practice this concept in your everyday conversations with your children. A few examples are listed below, and you can add others as you think of them during the day. You can make the games more interactive by asking your children to fill in the blanks.

Mealtime

"IF we are drinking juice, THEN we are NOT drinking
_____."

"IF this IS a hamburger, THEN it is NOT a
_____."

"IF we are sitting at this table, THEN we are NOT sitting on the _____."

Playtime

"IF Jamie IS painting, THEN he is NOT
_____."

"IF Carle IS building with blocks, THEN she is NOT
_____."

Events of the Day

"IF today IS Tuesday, THEN it is NOT
_____."

"IF it IS September, THEN it is NOT
_____."

"IF it IS raining outside today, THEN we can NOT play
_____."

Story Time

"IF the child in the story went to the circus, THEN he did NOT go to the _____."

"IF Cinderella did NOT get home by midnight, THEN she would _____."

Outdoors

"IF this rock is very heavy and I put it in the pond, THEN it will *(sink)* to the bottom."

"IF this plant does NOT get any water, THEN what will happen to it?"

Might/Maybe

The ICPS words *might* and *maybe* are used with the words *if* and *then* to build a still better understanding of consequential thinking. By combining these concepts, children can begin to think for themselves, "IF I choose this solution, THEN I MIGHT NOT get what I want and that would make me ANGRY." Or, "IF I do this, THEN my friend MIGHT NOT feel HAPPY."

Beyond recognizing and finding out about others' feelings, children can use these words to think about ways to influence those feelings. Considering people's preferences is the first step toward doing this, but young children often assume that others like the same things they do—an assumption often leading to faulty conclusions, and therefore unsuccessful solutions. The ICPS words *might* and *maybe* can be used to help children find out the preferences of others. In later problem solving, children will come to appreciate that offering another a doll, for example, in exchange for a shovel may not work because even though they themselves may like dolls, the other child *might not* like dolls.

◆　◆　◆

When the kids finished their puppet play, Marie called them into the kitchen. (At age two, Peter is too young to continue the ICPS word games, but he still loves to tag along and listen. Many times he repeats ICPS words and phrases after the big-

ger kids; in his own way he's preparing to be an ICPS thinker.)
As they all gathered around the table, Marie poured each one
a glass of juice and introduced the next ICPS word pair:
MIGHT/MAYBE.

Using Tanya's Ollie puppet, Marie began:

MOM: Okay, kids. Let's find out what Ollie likes to eat. Alison,
what do you think?

ALISON: He likes apples.

MOM: MAYBE he likes apples. MAYBE he does NOT like
apples. We have to find out. *Asking* is one way to find out.
Go ahead, Alex, ask him.

ALEX: Ollie, do you like apples?

OLLIE: No.

MOM: See, you *asked* him and he said no. Alex, what do you
think Ollie likes to eat?

ALEX: Candy.

MOM: MAYBE he likes candy. MAYBE he does NOT like
candy. How can you find out?

ALEX: Ask him.

MOM: Go ahead and ask him.

ALEX: *(to Ollie)* Do you like candy?

OLLIE: Yep.

MOM: Good, Alex. You *asked* him and you found out.

PETER: Me too!

MOM: Oh, Peter likes candy. Alex likes candy. Do Peter AND
Alex like the SAME thing OR something DIFFERENT?

CHILDREN: *(all excitedly chanting)* The SAME thing!

ALISON: I like candy too.

MOM: Oh, do ALL of you like candy, OR do SOME of you like
candy?

CHILDREN: *(all chiming in at once)* We ALL do.

MOM: If you gave Ollie some candy, would he like that?

CHILDREN: *(shouting together)* Yes!

MOM: He MIGHT like that. He MIGHT NOT like that. How can you find out?

ALEX: Ask him.

MOM: Go ahead and ask him.

ALISON: Ollie, do you like candy?

OLLIE: No!

ALEX: *(to Ollie)* Do you like bananas?

OLLIE: No!

ALEX: Do you like hamburgers?

OLLIE: No!

ALEX: Do you like potato chips?

OLLIE: Yep!

MOM: Alex, do you like potato chips?

ALEX: No.

MOM: Ollie likes potato chips. Alex likes candy. Do Ollie and Alex like the SAME thing OR something DIFFERENT?

CHILDREN: DIFFERENT.

MOM: Is it okay for DIFFERENT people to like DIFFERENT things?

CHILDREN: *(yelling at the same time)* Yes!

MOM: Yes, it IS okay for DIFFERENT people to like DIFFERENT things.

Marie wanted to use this puppet play to help her children think about how different people can like different things. As often happens during ICPS time, both Alex and Alison spontaneously added something to the activity that enhanced the fun and the objective. Alex got carried away with the phrase "Do you like?" and kept asking it over and over. His mom let him ask Ollie this question repeatedly because she knew ICPS is most successful when kids find their own enjoyable way to reinforce the concepts. Alison, too, grabbed on to the fun of the idea when she skipped away from the kitchen table chanting in a singsong voice, "Different people like different things. Different people like different things." This is ICPS in action.

◆ ◆ ◆

Can you see now how the words *might* and *maybe* help children think about the preferences of others and consider how other people feel? They help them think, "IF I hit Mikey, THEN he MIGHT get mad." Or, "IF I give my mother a hug, THEN MAYBE she'll feel happy." *Might* and *maybe* also help remind children that they cannot always know how people feel—sometimes they have to ask. Your children's understanding of the different emotions used in earlier activities will be reinforced now as they practice thinking about *might* and *maybe*. They can come to see that if one way does *not* make someone feel happy, it is possible to try a different way.

One day after school Alison and Alex were fighting. Alison was playing with her dolls, and Alex grabbed one and ran away with it. Marie thought this would be a good time to use an ICPS mini-dialogue to help them think about this problem. "Come over here by me," said Marie as she entered the room. "Let's use our two new ICPS words, MIGHT and MAYBE, to help you with this problem."

Alex and Alison quieted down and came over to sit by their mom. To Marie, this alone signaled an improvement in their behavior. Because they had come to associate ICPS time with enjoyable activities, they were willing to stop their arguing and listen to what she had to say. Marie didn't intend to solve their problem; she wanted only to make them think about each other's feelings when solving their own problems. She began:

MOM: What do each of you look like when you're HAPPY? *(Alex and Alison smiled.)*
MOM: Can you show me a SAD face? *(Alex and Alison made*

very sad faces and giggled as they watched each other pretend to feel sad.)

MOM: Alison, how do you look when you're ANGRY? *(Alison looked angry.)*

MOM: Alex, how do you look when you're ANGRY? *(Alex made an angry face.)*

MOM: Alison, do you like to play with dolls?

ALISON: Yes.

MOM: IF someone gave you a doll, how would that make you feel?

ALISON: Happy.

MOM: Okay. Now, let's imagine that Alison has a doll and someone snatches it way. Alex, how would that make Alison feel?

ALEX: ANGRY.

MOM: MAYBE it would make Alison ANGRY, OR MAYBE it would make her feel SAD. I said MAYBE because MAYBE means we don't know for sure. To find out how Alison would feel, let's ask her: Alison, IF someone snatched a doll from you, how would that make you feel?

ALISON: ANGRY.

MOM: Alex, how do you think Alison might feel IF that someone gave the doll back to Alison?

ALEX: HAPPY?

MOM: I don't know; let's ask her. Alison, would you feel HAPPY if someone gave the doll back to you?

ALISON: Yes.

MOM: I think that's very interesting that we can make someone else feel HAPPY, SAD, OR ANGRY.

This mini-dialogue didn't solve the problem of Alex grabbing things from his sister. But it did introduce into their real lives the use of two new ICPS words, and it helped these children think about the relationship between what they do and say and how other people feel.

Why/Because

The words *why* and *because* help children see the connection between an act and its consequences: "He hit me BECAUSE I took his toy." They also help children understand how a problem can be avoided: "I fell BECAUSE I ran too fast."

One day Tanya's mother was caring for Alison, Alex, and Peter while Marie was food shopping. After about an hour of playing very nicely together, Karena noticed that the kids seemed to be getting a bit restless. This, she thought, would be a perfect time to play an ICPS puppet game.

"Tanya," she called. "Get your puppets and let's play ICPS while we're waiting for Alison's mom to come home."

In just seconds all the kids and the puppets were in the living room. "Let me do it first," pleaded Alison.

"No, me!" demanded Alex.

"Could I have a turn?" asked Tanya.

"Wait. Calm down," said Tanya's mom while laughing at Peter, who had taken advantage of the moment of confusion to grab the puppets and begin his own game. "I'm going to let Ollie teach you some new ICPS words. Let me do one story and then you can each take a turn. Okay? Now sit down. Peter, give me the puppets and I'll start a puppet show about the words *why* and *because*."

OLLIE: Hi, I'm Ollie.
I came to play a game with you today.
I came to play the WHY/BECAUSE game.
Let me show you how to play.
First, I'll play with Mommy here. *(Karena turns the puppet toward herself.)* Mommy, I'm very tired.

PARENT: WHY?

OLLIE: BECAUSE I forgot to take my nap.

OLLIE: *(talking to the children)* Now I'm going to play with you. When I say something, you all ask very loud, WHY? Let's try it. I'm very hungry. Now you ask me, WHY?

CHILDREN: WHY?!

OLLIE: That was very good. Now, remember, ask WHY every time I say something.

I'm very hungry.

CHILDREN: WHY?

OLLIE: BECAUSE I haven't had my lunch.

OLLIE: I like going to school.

CHILDREN: WHY?

OLLIE: BECAUSE the children there are my friends.

OLLIE: I can't sing today.

CHILDREN: WHY?

OLLIE: BECAUSE my throat hurts.

OLLIE: You're doing very well! Now let's change the game. I'm going to ask you WHY and you make up the BE-CAUSE. Now listen. *(Ollie turns to Tanya's mom.)* I'm going to the store. I'm going to walk to the store; I'm NOT going to take the car or the bus. Can you guess WHY I'm going to walk?

PARENT: BECAUSE it's a nice day out.

OLLIE: MAYBE. Can you think of a DIFFERENT BECAUSE?

PARENT: BECAUSE your friend is walking to the store and you want to walk with your friend.

OLLIE: See, there is more than one BECAUSE. Now let's play together.

OLLIE: *(turning toward the children)* Johnny won't come to my house and play with me today. WHY won't Johnny come to my house and play with me today? Tanya, do you have a BECAUSE?

TANYA: *(shakes her head no)*

ALEX: *(yelling out)* BECAUSE he's sick!

OLLIE: MAYBE he's sick; Alison, can you think of another BECAUSE?

ALISON: BECAUSE his mother won't let him?

OLLIE: MAYBE. How about you, Tanya; can you think of a reason WHY Johnny won't come to my house?

TANYA: BECAUSE he doesn't like you.

At this response all the children fell over laughing wildly. Alison's mom walked in the door just at that moment and said, "It must be ICPS time."

There are many ways you can play with the ICPS words *why* and *because*. In addition to the puppet play above (adapted from my classroom curriculum guides *I Can Problem Solve*), the picture of the two children and the radio on page 78 can further help your children appreciate that two people can feel *different* ways about the *same* thing and that there are reasons why.

Show your children this picture and ask questions such as these:

"Do this boy *(point to the boy)* AND this girl *(point to the girl)* feel the SAME way OR a DIFFERENT way about listening to this music?"

"WHY might the girl feel HAPPY about listening to this music?"

"Any other reason? Another BECAUSE?"

"How does the boy feel about this?"

"WHY might he feel that way?"

"That's one BECAUSE (reason). Any other reason? Another BECAUSE?"

"Is it okay for DIFFERENT people to feel DIFFERENT ways about the SAME thing? Yes, it IS okay."

"How could the girl tell how the boy feels about the music?"

"Yes, she could turn around and see with her eyes. OR she could also ask."

Daily Use: Nonproblem Situations

You can practice *why* and *because* word games at any time of the day.

When You're Driving Your Children to School

"When I went to school, I especially liked Mondays. Can you guess WHY I liked Mondays?" Then let your children think of as many BECAUSES as they can.

When Wrapping a Gift for a Birthday Party

"This is the perfect gift for your friend. Can you guess WHY I think it's perfect?"

While Cooking

"Carrots are good for you. Can you guess WHY they're good for you?"

When Your Children Get into the Car

"It's important to wear seat belts. Do you know WHY?"

Fair/Not Fair

The final word pair in this pre–problem-solving stage is FAIR/NOT FAIR. These words help children understand the rights of others and self in decision making. Thinking ahead, Marie thought it would be a good idea to play with these words in a circumstance that realistically enacted a FAIR/NOT FAIR decision. She told her husband about her idea and encouraged him to introduce these words.

That night, the children ran into the kitchen looking for their bedtime snack. "Tonight," said their mom, "Dad is going to use your snacks to give you one more ICPS word. The new word is *FAIR*."

Sounding quite surprised, Alex exclaimed, "I forgot you know about ICPS!"

"Sure I do," said Dad. "Come here and listen."

DAD: *(while handing each child one cookie)* I have three oat-meal cookies. I have only enough for each of you to have one—one for Alison, one for Alex, and one for Peter.
Is that FAIR for each of you to have one cookie? Yes, it IS FAIR for each of you to have the SAME number.

(Taking Peter's cookie and giving it to Alison) IF Alison wants two cookies and I give her two, THEN Alex would have only one and Peter would have none.

Is that FAIR?

No. That's NOT FAIR.

Alison, how do you think Alex and Peter MIGHT feel if I let you eat those two cookies?

ALISON: ANGRY.

DAD: Yes, they MIGHT feel ANGRY.

Alex, can you use the new ICPS word to tell me WHY you MIGHT feel ANGRY?

ALEX: Because that's NOT FAIR.

DAD: Good thinking. So here you are—one cookie for each of you. Now, that's FAIR.

This conversation took only a minute but it established *fair* and *not fair* as ICPS words; it began to get dad more involved with this approach; and it reinforced Alison and Alex's concept of the word *fair*.

Tanya's mom also used a personal experience in Tanya's day to introduce the word *fair*. Tanya came home from school complaining that a boy in her class would not let her share the clay during indoor recess.

MOM: Let's talk about the word *FAIR*. IF something belongs to the school and one child takes ALL of the turns—that means other children do NOT get any turns—that is NOT FAIR. Can you tell me what IS FAIR?

TANYA: To take turns.

MOM: Okay. Now let's talk about the clay. Did Sean use ALL of the clay OR SOME of the clay?

TANYA: All of the clay.

MOM: Can you think of what would be FAIR?

TANYA: I wanted it.

MOM: Would it be FAIR for each of you to have SOME of the clay OR for one of you to have ALL of it?

TANYA: Each of us to have SOME.

MOM: What can you say to Sean the next time he won't share the clay?

TANYA: You take some and give me some. That's FAIR.

Whether Tanya would feel assertive enough to really say this to Sean is not the issue. Even though Tanya was already familiar with the word *fair*, she now had a new way to help her think about its meaning in a conflict situation and how to use it in a nonthreatening way. When she's ready, she will have one more concept to help her solve her problems.

◆ ◆ ◆

Opportunities to use the word *fair* as a basis for decision making are all around you. Once you introduce the word as an ICPS concept, try to reinforce the idea in your daily conversations in both nonproblem and problem situations.

Daily Use: Nonproblem Situations

Events of the Day

"Did you do anything today that was NOT FAIR?"

"What could you have done to be FAIR?"

"Did anyone do anything to you today that was NOT FAIR?"

"What could this person have done to be FAIR?"

Story Time

"Is what happened in this story FAIR or NOT FAIR?"

"WHY do you think that?"

(if NOT FAIR): "What could have happened that would be FAIR?"

ICPS Mini-Dialogues: Problem Situations

When a Child Wants All Your Attention

"Is it FAIR for you to have ALL my attention and your younger sister NOT to have any?"

"How do you think Kim feels when she wants a chance to talk to me but you keep shouting out AND interrupting?"

When a Child Refuses to Take Turns or Share

"Is it FAIR for you to have ALL the turns and for your friends NOT to have any?"

"How MIGHT your friend feel if you do NOT let him play with that?"

"You played with that BEFORE. Jannette did NOT have a turn with it. Is it FAIR for you to play NOW? Can you think of something DIFFERENT to do NOW?"

"Did your brother finish his turn with that? Is it FAIR for you to take that BEFORE he has finished a turn?"

"Is it FAIR for you to have your turn BEFORE or AF-TER he has finished a turn?"

With the word concepts now well ingrained in their daily conversations and activities, these kids were ready to problem solve the ICPS way.

You may now wish to add the additional ICPS word pairs to your list.

GOOD TIME/NOT A GOOD TIME
IF/THEN
MIGHT/MAYBE
WHY/BECAUSE
FAIR/NOT FAIR

5

◆ ● ◆

Finding Alternative Solutions

By this time you probably feel quite comfortable using ICPS vocabulary words when you talk to your kids during the day. Your children are also likely to be so familiar with ICPS concepts that they naturally look at problem situations a bit differently and think more often about how feelings affect these problems. In fact, in many homes, ICPS works so well up to this point that parents sometimes feel content to stop right here. They can see that their kids have changed the way they think about problems, and they feel the whole family now knows enough about ICPS to use it without adding more activities, games, or exercises.

Although I'm always happy to see parents feeling successful and happy with their children's progress, I have to caution them that it's not time to stop learning ICPS. The skills practiced so far support only pre–problem-solving thinking. That's why ICPS conversations thus far have been called mini-dialogues. They're not complete. The most important part of ICPS—the part where children actually learn to solve their problems—is yet to come in finding alternative solutions and considering consequences.

In Chapter Two when Alison and Alex were arguing over who had the toy first, you may remember that the emphasis was on ICPS word concepts that set the stage for solving the problem. Marie began by asking, in a nonthreatening tone,

"What's going on?" When each child answered, "I had it first," Marie didn't try to decipher who really did have it first because she would never really know. She simply used another ICPS concept to acknowledge that grabbing was one way to get the toy back, and then asked, "What happened AFTER you grabbed?" When Alison replied that they started fighting, Marie asked if either of them could think of a different way to play so they wouldn't have to fight.

Even in the earliest stages of using ICPS word concepts, the children came up with solutions to their problems. But that was only the beginning because first solutions may not always be appropriate or successful.

At another time, a similar problem came up, and as usual, Alex and Alison echoed the familiar chant, "I had it first." This time Marie used the ICPS word concepts in a new way:

MOM: What happened? What's the problem?

ALEX: I had it first.

ALISON: I had it first.

MOM: Do you two see what happened the SAME way OR a DIFFERENT way?

ALEX: A different way.

MOM: One of you had the toy BEFORE the other. Is it FAIR for one of you to have the toy ALL of the time?
(Mom added guidance about feelings to her mini-dialogue.)

ALISON: No.

MOM: Alex, how MIGHT Alison feel if you have the toy ALL of the time?

ALEX: Mad.

MOM: Alison, how might Alex feel if you have the toy ALL of the time?

ALISON: ANGRY.

MOM: We still have a problem here. Can either of you think of something DIFFERENT to do so you both won't feel ANGRY?

Children's understanding of other people's feelings is an important component of dialoguing. Being aware that what they do might make another feel angry is a step ahead of being insensitive to others' feelings. But that is still not enough. If children do not know what to do about that anger, they could become even more upset, react aggressively, or perhaps freeze over the fear of another's anger. That's why this next set of activities focusing on thinking about alternative solutions is so important. Although Alex and Alison did come up with a solution to this problem early on and developed sensitivity to each other's feelings, it's also important that children learn to think, "IF my first way does NOT work, THEN I can try a DIFFERENT way."

Marie and her family are ready to move out of the preparatory pre–problem-solving stage of ICPS and into the problem-solving arena. Although they'll still occasionally use the games and activities of earlier chapters to review and practice ICPS concepts, they'll now expand the dialogues to find multiple solutions to the problems they run into in their daily interactions with other people.

The Process of Finding Alternative Solutions

The activities in this chapter will help your children learn that there is more than one way to solve a problem. In particular, they will be encouraged to think of as many different solutions as possible to everyday interpersonal problems; this will help them develop a process of thinking that says, "There's more than one way; I don't have to use the first idea I think of, or give up so soon."

It's best to begin this process using pretend children and circumstances; this introduces the idea in a nonthreatening way. Using puppets, pictures, and role playing, the general procedure for eliciting alternative solutions follows this pattern:

1. State the problem or have the child state the problem.
2. Say that the idea is to think of lots of *different* ways to solve this problem.
3. Write down all the ideas. (Even though your young children may not be able to read, they like to see you write down what they say.)
4. Ask for the first solution. If the solution is relevant, repeat it and identify it as one way to solve the problem. Remind your children that the object is to think of lots of *different* ways to solve the problem.
5. Ask for another solution, and so forth.
6. If solution ideas run out too quickly, probe for more by asking, "What can you *say* to solve this problem?" Or, "What can you *do* to solve this problem?"

When you begin helping your children find alternative solutions, try presenting the idea in a conversation that sounds something like this one between Marie and Alex and Alison:

MOM: Let's pretend that a six-year-old girl wants her brother to let her use his video game. To help this girl get a chance to play with the video game, let's play the "What Else Can She Do?" game. We want to think of lots of ways, lots of DIFFERENT solutions to this problem. As you think of them, I'll write them down on this paper. Alex, can you think of a way that the girl can get her brother to let her use the video game?

ALEX: She could tell her mother.

MOM: Okay *(writing that down)*, she could tell her mother. That's *one* way. Now, the idea of this game is to think of lots of DIFFERENT ways this girl can get her brother to let her use his video game. Who's got way number two? Let's fill up the paper.

ALISON: She could let him play with her toys.

MOM: *(writing that down)* She could tell her mother OR she could let him play with her toys. Now we have two ways. Alex, can you think of way number three? *(holding up three fingers very dramatically)*

ALEX: She could let him play with her toys.

MOM: Oh, that's the SAME idea Alison had. I bet you can think of a DIFFERENT way.

ALEX: She could say, "Please, please, can I play with your game?"

MOM: *(writing that down)* You're thinking of lots of DIFFERENT ways. Who can tell us another way, way number four?

ALISON: She could cry.

MOM: She *could* cry.

> *(This is an unclear response. It could be a mere reaction to not having her wish, or it could be a concerted attempt to manipulate the other's feelings. Marie asks for more information.)*

Tell me more about that.

ALISON: So he will feel sorry for her.

MOM: Okay. *(In this case, crying is a solution, so Marie writes it down.)* Now you have four ways. Let's fill up this whole paper with lots of DIFFERENT ideas. Remember, that's the idea of the game.

ALEX: Give him some candy.
(Adding to the list)

ALEX: Wait till he's not looking and then take it.
MOM: You thought of six DIFFERENT ways the girl could try
to get her brother to let her use his video game.
(Reading off the list)

1. "She could tell her mother."
2. "She could let him play with her toys."
3. "She could say, 'Please, please, can I play with your
   game?' "
4. "She could cry so he'll feel sorry for her."
5. "She could give him candy."
6. "She could wait till he's not looking and then take it."

MOM: You thought of lots of ideas. How do you feel about
that—PROUD or FRUSTRATED?
ALEX AND ALISON: PROUD!

Because the purpose of this lesson-game is to guide children
to think of more than one way to solve a problem, the thinking
process is more important right now than the content of their
solutions. You may have wondered why Marie didn't react
when Alex suggested, "Wait till he's not looking and then take
it." It is very tempting to explain why that idea isn't a good
one, and you might become concerned that children will be
encouraged to think of unacceptable ways to obtain what they
want. In the next chapter, you'll see how the child will be
guided to consider consequences and whether an idea *is* or *is
not* a good one. But at this point it's important to let the child
be free to think. Reacting to the content of a particular solution
could inhibit that freedom.

You can give your children practice at using this freedom to find alternative solutions with many different make-believe problems. Some problems you might help your children try to solve include:

- A girl at the top of the slide wants the boy at the bottom to get off so she can slide down.
- A boy wants to play with a ball his friend is playing with.
- A girl wants to roller skate with a neighborhood child, but the child doesn't want to skate.
- A boy wants to watch a TV show, but his sister is already watching a different show.

You can also let your children make up their own problem stories, or find them in pictures from story books, magazines, or newspapers.

Helpful Hints

Hint No. 1: Keeping Solutions Coming

Kids generally think there's only one right answer to a question, so at first they may be confused when you ask for a different idea after they've already offered one solution. Your children may think their first response was "wrong" when you ask, "Can you think of a DIFFERENT way to solve that problem?" To encourage more solutions and flexibility of thought, before you ask for a second solution you might say, "That's *one* way. Now, the idea of this game is to think of lots of DIFFERENT ways." Then ask for another solution. This validates the first response and reminds the child that asking for a different way is part of the game.

Hint No. 2: Handling Irrelevant or Seemingly Irrelevant Responses

Sometimes a child may respond to your request for more solutions by offering a solution that is irrelevant to the problem. In the story above, for example, Alison's solution "She could cry" was intended to gain sympathy (it is a *cognitive cry*) and therefore it was a valid solution. But if she had said that the girl could cry because she can't play with the video game, the response would have been irrelevant because it's a reaction to frustration, not a way to solve the problem.

When this happens, acknowledge the answer without writing it down on your list, and then clarify for your child what it is you're looking for. In this case, the parent might say: "She MIGHT cry, but in this game we're looking for a way the girl can get a chance to play with the video game."

At other times, a response may seem to be irrelevant from your viewpoint, but if you ask for clarification you may find it is actually an acceptable solution. What if Alex had suggested that the girl could get to use the video game if she got her mother's wallet? This would at first seem irrelevant to solving the problem. But if Marie asked, "How could that solve the problem?" Alex might explain, "So she could give the boy a quarter to have a turn." Now it's a solution. (This kind of response will be evaluated by the child in the lessons in Chapter Six.)

Hint No. 3: Handling Enumerations (Variations on a Theme)

Enumerations occur when children offer solutions that, although different in detail, repeat the theme of an earlier answer. For example, one child may solve the problem above by saying, "Tell her mother." The same or a different child may pick up on this surreptitious theme and say, "Tell her father."

When this happens, group the answers into a single category on your list and then ask for something *different*. In this case, the parent might say, "Telling her mother and telling her father are kind of the SAME BECAUSE they are both *telling someone*. Can you think of something DIFFERENT from telling someone?"

Other examples of enumerations include:

> *Giving something:* Give him candy, give him gum, and so on.

> *Hurting someone:* Hit him, kick him, bite him, etc.

> *Using emotions:* Cry, whine, look sad, etc.

You should also be careful how you respond to given solutions because you might actually encourage enumerations. Saying, "That's a good idea" makes your child think that if you like the solution "give him candy," for example, you'll also like "give him gum" and "give him potato chips," and all variations on the theme "give him something." If you find yourself saying, "Good" (and most of us do), you can reinforce the *process* by saying, "Good, you thought of something DIFFERENT," or, "Good, you thought of an idea."

ICPSing in Action

Not long after you introduce this concept, you may be pleasantly surprised to hear your children using this thinking skill without prompting from you.

Marie's first glimpse into Alison's understanding of alternative solutions came rather abruptly after hearing the sound of breaking glass. By the time Marie arrived on the scene in the backyard, Alison's father was standing over his daughter yelling in anger. "I've told you a hundred times not to throw a hard ball near the house!" he screamed. "Now are you happy? The kitchen window is broken and I've got to pay to get it fixed!"

"I'm sorry," said Alison. "I could save my allowance to pay for it, or maybe I could call Grandpa and he could fix it."

Marie could tell that her husband was too angry to remember that ICPS dialogues are not just for fun, but for solving problems too, so she quickly jumped in to help Alison continue finding solutions to her problem.

"Alison, it's good to hear you thinking of DIFFERENT ways to solve this problem," her mom interrupted. "Why don't you back up and first tell us what happened."

"Well, I didn't really do it. Ryan threw the ball real hard at me, but it was over my head and I couldn't catch it. Then it broke the window and he ran away."

"How do you think Ryan felt when he broke the window and ran away?"

"He was afraid."

"How did *you* feel?"

"I was mad at him, but then Dad came out and I got scared."

"WHY did you get scared if you didn't break the window?"

"Because he told me not to play ball near the house."

"How do you think Dad feels about this?"

"Mad."

Alison began to cry as she added, "But I told him I would help pay for it or ask Grandpa to fix it."

"I heard you," said her mom. "What else MIGHT you do so Dad won't be so upset?"

"I could promise not to do it again," offered Alison through her tears.

"That's another idea," agreed Mom.

Alison's dad had been standing to the side listening to this dialogue. It was hard for him to always respond to problems with ICPS because he wasn't as actively involved with the games and activities as Marie, but at that moment, he was very impressed. The normal course of his discipline style would have followed the predictable pattern of dad yelling, child crying, and everybody feeling upset and angry. Here in less than one minute, ICPS had helped clarify what really happened, established that Alison understood why her father was angry, and prompted her to offer her own solutions to her problem. The results were hard to argue with.

"Alison," said her dad, "I am very angry about the broken window. But I'm also glad to hear that you understand how I feel and are willing to think of a way to solve the problem. I'll tell you what—I accept your apology and your promise not to play ball here again, and I also would like you to call Grandpa and ask him if he could come over to help me fix the window."

Alison walked away from this "disaster" feeling proud of herself. She had learned her lesson about playing ball near the house, and she had also learned that ICPS really does help solve problems.

Marie had been playing ICPS games and using ICPS mini-dialogues with her children for several weeks when the broken window incident occurred. Although not all children will think of alternative solutions on their own so soon after they first play the games, Alison did pick up on ICPS's practical use right away. "I was just amazed," said her mom. "I know she and Alex both enjoy the games and they recognize the words when I use them in problem situations, but this was the first time I could see for myself the way ICPS really does help kids think about the problem and how to solve it."

Before ICPS Alison wouldn't have realized that the problem wasn't the broken window (which she didn't actually break) but rather her disobedience in playing ball where she had been told not to. Without thinking about what she did or how her dad felt, Alison would have either argued with her dad because she "didn't do it," or she would have run off crying to her room. Neither solution would have worked to resolve the conflict like the ICPS solution.

Feeling Too Angry to Dialogue

If you find yourself yelling at your children (like Alison's dad) or ranting on and on about their disobedient or inconsiderate actions, don't conclude that ICPS isn't for you. It's not uncommon for parents to fall back on old habits when they're too angry to think clearly enough to dialogue. This is particularly true if the child creates the same problem over and over or breaks an object of special value. Because parental emotions are usually part of the problem for the child to think about, sometimes you'll find it best to delay ICPS dialoguing when you are very upset yourself. In these cases, clearly express your angry feelings, perhaps send your child to his or her room, and then later initiate an ICPS dialogue when you've calmed down. All is not lost in such circumstances, just delayed a bit.

There may be times when children are also too angry or upset to think about ICPSing. I remember a kindergarten girl who wanted her classmate to share the clay. When the classmate refused, the little girl (who had learned ICPS and was usually very good at solving her problems) began to cry. Through her sobbing tears she could barely tell her teacher what was the matter. It seems she wasn't upset that she couldn't play with the clay; she was hurt because she had always shared with this classmate and now, "she won't share with me." The teacher knew this wasn't the time to begin an ICPS dialogue. This child first needed to be comforted.

If you find your children in the middle of a problem that has made them very angry or distressed, don't try to solve the problem with ICPS right away. Wait until later in the day when they are calmer and more ready to think about what happened, how they felt about it, and the many ways they might have solved it.

What's Really the Problem?

When Marie and Tanya's mother, Karena, compared notes on their progress with solution finding, Karena admitted that she had found herself falling into a bad habit. It seems she had a tendency to ask for alternative solutions without using the pre–problem-solving concepts first. "I like this idea of helping Tanya think about ways to solve her own problems," she told Marie. "But I have to remember to start the dialogue by first finding out what the problem is and how she and others feel about it, and then asking for solutions."

You too may fall into this pattern because as a parent you're accustomed to being the one who defines the problem. Let's imagine that you walk into the kitchen and see your child standing over a spilled container of milk. Wanting to encourage ICPS thinking skills, you ask, "Now, how are you going to solve this problem?" The solutions your child might offer may confuse or annoy you if your child has a whole different idea of what the problem is. Your child might feel that the problem is the fact that the container is too large for him to hold; you, on the other hand, might be thinking more about the problem of the mess on the floor.

To show your children (and to remind yourself) how solution finding depends on each person's view of the problem, take a look at the illustration on page 98.

There are several possible interpretations of what the problem might be, and who is having it. One child may believe the girl wants her mom to buy her the doll, but her mom has said no and won't even look at her. Another child may assume the parents are yelling at the boy standing between them. A third may think the boy on the right wants those blocks and his father isn't paying any attention to him. It is even possible that someone may attribute the problem to either or both of the parents.

To experience the possible different interpretations of the illustration, and the need to find out what the problem is before guiding the child to think of ways to solve it, you can play the following game with your child or children.

PARENT: *(Duplicate this picture for child to draw on.)* Look at this picture and find a person who has a problem. Draw a face on that person that shows how you think he feels.

(When child is finished drawing): Tell me about the problem you see in the picture.

(After the child names the problem): I see another problem. *(Draw a sad face on another person in the picture and name the problem.)* Do you and I see the SAME problem OR a DIFFERENT problem?

Sometimes we think we know what the problem is just by looking; you know, by seeing with our _____ *(point to eyes).*

If these were real people, how else could we find out about the problem?

(Guide child to remember that we can listen to them or ask them): Let's try to solve the problem that you named. Who has the problem?

(Let child respond)

What can that person do to solve this problem?

(Let child respond)

That's *one* way; what's another way?

(Continue until the child runs out of ideas. Then repeat with the problem that you named.)

When Alison broke the window in her house, the problem would have never been solved to everyone's satisfaction if her

parents focused on the problem of disobedience, while she insisted, "But I didn't break it!" The game above will help you and your children remember to find out first who has the problem and what the problem is before anyone can begin to solve it.

Marie remembered this lesson a few weeks later when she noticed a pile of garbage under Alex's bed. Alex's Saturday chore was to empty his wastebasket into the garbage can in the basement, but apparently he had been emptying the trash under his bed instead. Before ICPS Marie would have angrily called Alex into the bedroom and scolded him fiercely for pulling such a stunt. "Get this garbage out of here this minute," she might have yelled, "and don't you ever put your trash under your bed again!" She also would have reminded him about responsibility: "It's your job to throw out your own trash. You have to learn to share the chores if you're going to be part of this family." But listen how, as an ICPS mom, Marie changed her approach with surprising results:

MOM: *(calmly)* Alex, why is this trash under your bed?

ALEX: 'CAUSE I don't like to take it down in the basement.

MOM: *(looking for Alex's view of the problem)* Why not?

ALEX: 'CAUSE I don't like to go down there alone; it makes me scared.

MOM: You never told me that.

ALEX: I was afraid you'd think I was a baby.

MOM: Alex, you don't have to empty your trash if it makes you feel afraid. But you are a part of this family, and I want you to do something to help take care of this house. Can you think of a way you can help?

(Marie identifies the real problem—handling responsibility—and guides Alex to think of a solution.)

ALEX: I can feed the fish.

MOM: Fine.
> *(Marie accepts Alex's preference*
> *as a solution to this problem.)*

Often beginning talk with "WHY did you . . . ?" is a signal of anger that the child knows is not a genuine request for information. But when questions are asked in a less threatening, information-seeking tone of voice, and the child's answer is heard, valuable insight can be gained. By taking time to identify the real problem, both Marie and Alex found a satisfactory solution. Alex was very proud of his decision to take care of the fish and he therefore did the job conscientiously; Marie was content because her son was learning to handle responsibility.

Role Playing

The broken window incident and the trash problem gave Marie renewed enthusiasm to continue the ICPS program with more solution-finding games. The first game she tried involved a bit of role playing to stress the need to get information before making assumptions and to reinforce the idea that there is more than one way to solve a problem.

The next day, Marie gathered Alex, Alison, and Tanya into the living room right after supper. "Let's play a new ICPS guessing game," she said. "Everyone will act out a scene and then I'll ask you questions about it." Marie instructed Alison and Tanya to stand together and pretend they were playing. She told Alex to walk up to the girls and just stand there. Then she instructed Tanya to look at Alex and shake her head no, and she told Alex to walk away looking sad.

"Who can guess what this problem is?" asked Mom.

"They wouldn't play with me," said Alex.

"What can Alex do OR say to get to play with others?" asked Mom.

"He could bring one of his toys to share with us," offered Alison.

"Good, you thought of way number one. Who can think of way number two?"

"I could scream at them until they let me," said Alex.

"That's a DIFFERENT way," said Mom. "Tanya, can you think of a third way?"

"He could tell the teacher," suggested Tanya.

"That's another way," Mom said with a smile.

Marie was able to act out problem situations because she had a room full of eager players, but this role-playing game can be practiced with only one child with the help of puppets. Hold two puppets and introduce them to your child as sister and brother puppets who have a problem. Act out a scene like the one that follows and ask your child to guess what the problem is.

SISTER: *(reading a book)*

BROTHER: *(starts to bump into and bother his sister)*

SISTER: Stop it!

BROTHER: *(continues to push against his sister)*

SISTER: Cut it out!

BROTHER: No.

PARENT: *(to child)* Can you guess what the problem is?
(Your child will respond with some version of "The brother won't leave the sister alone." Then let the sister puppet ask your child:)

SISTER: What can I do to get my brother to leave me alone while I'm reading my book?

When your children offer a solution, acknowledge the idea and then ask for a *different* way, and then a third way too. You can use the puppets to role-play many different problem situations that will give your kids practice at thinking of alternative solutions.

More Helpful Hints

Hint No. 4: Handling Parroters

When more than one child is playing ICPS solution-finding games, it's quite common for them to repeat (or parrot) one another's ideas when you ask for more possible solutions. Back in the dialogue about the girl and the video game, Alex repeated Alison's solution "She could let him play with her toys." When children like Alex, who are generally verbal, parrot another's response, you might respond as Marie did by saying, "Oh, I bet you can think of something DIFFERENT."

Children who parrot because they are generally inhibited nonresponders should not yet be pushed for a different idea. Rather, praise this child for having said something with a comment like, "I'm glad you told us that, too." Or you might let this child hold a puppet and ask the puppet for an idea, or encourage the very resistant child to whisper an idea into the puppet's ear.

Hint No. 5: Handling Dominating Behavior

If you ask for solutions from a group of children, but one child continually dominates the conversation and won't let others have a chance to think of solutions for themselves, you might ask the dominating child, "Is it FAIR for one child to have ALL the turns and for SOME NOT to have any?" Asking an ICPS-trained child to think about how others feel about his or her behavior is usually a good solution to this problem.

Puppet Play

Tanya's mom still used the puppets Tippy and Ollie to play ICPS games with Tanya, especially when she was at home without Alison or Alex. On their first day of playing with solution finding, they played the following puppet game. You might try something like this yourself to encourage shy or resistant children to think of different solutions.

TIPPY: *(starts to take the last cookie)*
OLLIE: I want that.
TIPPY: No, you already had one. I want it.
PARENT: What's happening? What's the matter?
OLLIE: Tippy's taking *my* cookie.
TIPPY: No, I'm not. Ollie's got *my* cookie.
PARENT: Do you two see what happened the SAME way OR a DIFFERENT way?
TIPPY: A DIFFERENT way.
PARENT: Oh, that means we have a problem. Can any of us think of a way to solve this problem?
OLLIE: I can't think of a way. Can you help me, Tanya?
TANYA: You could ask your mother if she has more.
PARENT: That's *one* way. The idea of this game is to think of lots of ways. What's a new way, a DIFFERENT way?
TANYA: You could break the cookie in half.
PARENT: Okay. That's a DIFFERENT way. I bet you can think of a third way.
TANYA: One of you can eat the cookie and the other can have something else like candy.
PARENT: Now Tippy and Ollie have three ways to try to solve their problem.
OLLIE: Thank you, Tanya.
TIPPY: Yeah, thanks. I'm gonna try all three ways!

Shy children like Tanya will find it difficult to think of ways to solve their own problems at first and so puppet play like this gives these children an opportunity to practice the idea in nonthreatening and nonpersonal ways. As their confidence in solution finding grows, so will their willingness to apply the thinking skills to their own problems.

In fact, a week or so after Tanya and her mom played these solution-finding games, Tanya's teacher commented to Karena that she'd noticed a change in the way Tanya handled herself with other children. In particular she remembered an instance where Tanya was watching two girls jumping rope on the playground. Obviously Tanya wanted to join them, but in her usual shy way she just stood nearby watching. "All of a sudden," the teacher told Karena, "Tanya walked up to the girl with the rope and said, 'If you need somebody to hold the other end of the rope, I could do it.' The two girls thought about the idea for a second or two and then gave Tanya one end of the rope and the three of them played happily for the rest of recess. I was so happy to see Tanya speak up and suggest an idea like that."

Had the *teacher* suggested that Tanya hold the rope, would the children have invited her to play? If they had, would Tanya have been ready? This time Tanya was ready—it was *her* idea.

ICPS Games for Solution Finding

Tic-Tac-Toe

Try a practice game of tic-tac-toe with your children to be sure they understand how the game is ordinarily played. Then announce that you know how to play ICPS tic-tac-toe: "I'm going to tell you a problem. If you can think of a DIFFERENT solution to the problem, you can put your mark—an O or an X—in a box. You'll skip your turn if you can't think of a solution or if you name a solution that has already been said."

You might start with a problem like this: Gary borrowed

Karl's new yo-yo and lost it. He's afraid Karl will be angry. What can Gary do or say so Karl won't be angry?

If you're playing with one child, you will be the opponent offering different solutions. If you're playing with two children, let them play against each other. If you're playing with more than two children, let them take turns.

Remember, let the children put an X or O in the box only if they have given a new and relevant solution. Enumerations and irrelevant responses don't count.

Storybook Game

You can use a storybook that presents an interpersonal problem to help your children practice finding alternative solutions. As you read the story, stop at appropriate places to ask questions like these:

"What happened? What's the problem?"

"Does anyone in the story see a DIFFERENT problem?"

"How do you think [Character #1] felt when _____ (repeat the problem)?"

"Do you think [Character #2] felt the SAME way OR a DIFFERENT way?"

"What did [Character #1] do or say to solve the problem?"

"How did [Character #2] feel when [Character #1] did or said that?"

"Can you think of a DIFFERENT way [Character #1] could have solved this problem?"

"Can you think of another DIFFERENT way?"

Puppet Play

You can use puppet play in a number of ways. It can encourage role playing in problem situations; the puppets can prompt resistant children to offer more solutions, and shy children can use puppets to speak for them.

The following puppet play, adapted from a classroom lesson I developed for the curriculum guides *I Can Problem Solve,* will give you an idea of how puppets can help children practice finding many different solutions to problem situations.

OLLIE: Mommy, Tippy poked me in the eye.

TIPPY: I did not. You poked *me* in the eye.

MOM: What happened BEFORE anyone got poked in the eye?

OLLIE: I was waiting for you to go outside and Tippy poked me in the eye with her jacket.

TIPPY: I did not!

MOM: Tippy, what do you think happened?

TIPPY: I was putting on my jacket, and it flew up when I went to put it on and it hit Ollie. Then Ollie poked me in the eye. It really hurt.

MOM: Did you try to hurt Ollie?

TIPPY: No.

MOM: Ollie, how do you feel now?

OLLIE: ANGRY.

MOM: And Tippy, how do you feel?

TIPPY: FRUSTRATED.

MOM: What is something you can do so Ollie is NOT ANGRY and Tippy is NOT FRUSTRATED? *(To your own child or children)* How can we solve this problem?

CHILD: Tell you.

MOM: Yes, they could. Can you think of a DIFFERENT way? A way they can solve this problem themselves?

CHILD: They could talk it out.

MOM: That's *one* way. Can you think of a DIFFERENT way?
CHILD: They could say, "Let's be friends again."
MOM: That's another way. Can you think of way number three?
CHILD: They could give each other presents.
MOM: You did a good job of thinking of DIFFERENT ways
Tippy and Ollie could solve their problem.

The puppet plays and games of ICPS are a fun way to practice skills that will have their most helpful role in solving real-life problems. Most children enjoy the games and can think about other people's feelings and a variety of different solutions in these situations long before they begin applying them to their daily problems. So have patience. Spend lots of time playing the games and prompting your children to use ICPS thinking skills when they have a problem—then keep your eyes and ears open for signs of ICPS in the way your children think about their own problems.

Even Alex, whose style of solving problems had always been impulsive and aggressive, surprised his mom one day with an ICPS solution. After several weeks of playing solution-finding games, Alex used the skills to get his mother to buy him a candy bar while they were shopping in the grocery store.

"Can I have this candy?" Alex asked.

"No," said his mom in her usual way.

"Pleeeease," Alex began to whine in his usual way.

"No," repeated his mom.

"It would make me feel happy," tried Alex.

This use of a feeling word caught Marie's attention. Stifling a smile, she said, "Oh, would it really make you HAPPY?"

"Yeah," said Alex in earnest. "And I won't eat it until after dinner."

"I couldn't believe it," Marie told me later. "I almost dropped a whole chicken on the floor. Alex and I have been through this crying-for-candy routine a thousand times before.

But to hear him start to think of other ways besides crying and whining to get what he wanted was just amazing. Of course, I couldn't resist—I bought him the candy and he really did wait until after dinner to eat it. There will still be times when the answer is 'No' no matter how many solutions he thinks of, but at that moment in the grocery store I could see that this ICPS way of looking at problems was really going to help Alex stop being so nagging and demanding."

Alex surely was learning the skills of ICPS thinking and he often showed a willingness to consider alternative solutions. However, he was not yet a complete ICPS problem solver. Although he could think of alternative solutions with his mom, the solutions he chose to act on with his friends were still quite frequently aggressive (remember his solution to get the girls to let him play: "I could scream at them until they let me") or irrelevant (like the idea to take money from his mother's wallet to get a chance to play a video game). But at the time he offered those solutions, they were accepted by his mother as part of the brainstorming game. Up to this point in ICPS, like Alex, your children have been free to think of solutions to problems without evaluating their content—without judgment. Once your children develop this habit of thinking that "there's more than one way," they can then move on to the next chapter to consider "what MIGHT happen next IF I do that?"

6

Considering Consequences

Up to now, your children have practiced thinking of different solutions to pretend and real problems. You'll remember that when Tanya, Alison, and Alex role played a scene in which they portrayed two children who wouldn't let a third child play, they were able to think of several possible solutions to the problem—and even Alex's suggestion to "scream until they let me" was not disparaged because ICPS is process more than content. We're now going to add the final problem-solving skill—consequential thinking—so your children can learn to evaluate the impact of their solutions on themselves and others. It's difficult for children to think simultaneously about what they could do and what might happen if they do that, but I have learned over the years that children as young as four can become quite good at this in time.

It's this last step that makes ICPS problem solving so valuable to your children both now and as they grow. The people in our society who repeatedly respond to their problems with others in insensitive, cruel, or destructive ways haven't grown up in the habit of thinking about the consequences of their solutions before they act. ICPS-trained individuals, on the other hand, are better able to respond to their daily conflicts in reasonable and responsible ways because they have practiced the skill of consequential thinking.

Thinking About the Sequence of Things

The goal of consequential thinking is to help your children think about what might happen *next* if a particular solution is carried out. Therefore, consequences make sense only when children know that events follow one another in a certain order. Your children will be able to meet this goal more easily if you first review the idea that things happen in a certain sequence.

Before and After

Sequential thinking can be reviewed by looking back in Chapter Two at the word games for *before* and *after.* These words allow children to recognize a consequential situation such as, "He hit me AFTER I called him a name."

You can practice this concept with your children while you're doing any two-step process—like preparing a bowl of cereal ("I pour on the milk AFTER I put the cereal in the bowl") or brushing your teeth ("I put toothpaste on my brush BEFORE I clean my teeth"). Then let your children make up examples of their own.

Story Building

Story building is another sequential game that's lots of fun and can be played almost anytime or anywhere—while you're doing the dishes, driving the car, or waiting on line at the supermarket. Give this a try:

Start story building by making up a story about anything at all and then let your children take turns finishing it. Marie started her story-building game with Alex in this way:

"Once upon a time," she said, "a little boy's mother wanted to bake a cake. So the first thing she did was mix ALL the

ingredients together. Then she . . ." Marie stopped and asked
Alex to fill in what happened next.

"Then she put it in the oven," he said.

Marie picked up the story. "And then it baked. What do
you think happened next?"

"Then she gave the cake to her little boy and he ate it all
up!" giggled Alex.

You can use stories like Marie's that have well-known steps
like planting a garden or setting the table, or you can build
more imaginative open-ended stories like one that might begin: "Once upon a time a little girl moved to a new house.
When she arrived, the first thing she did was . . ." and then ask
what happens next in the story. This helps children give
thoughtful consideration to the question "What happens
next?"

What Might Happen If . . .

You can also review the idea of sequence with a game called
"What MIGHT Happen IF . . ." In this game, you give your
children the circumstance and let them fill in the consequence.
You can try the following few statements for starters and then
make up more of your own:

"What MIGHT happen IF . . .

• you stayed up all night without going to sleep?"
• you wore a bathing suit in the snow?"
• a person never brushed his teeth?"
• a woman never fed her pet?"
• a child ate only junk food?"
• it never rained?"

These games that practice sequential thinking will promote
your children's willingness to consider: "IF I choose this so-

lution, what MIGHT happen next?" This "what MIGHT happen next" is the consequence that's so important to effective problem solving.

Considering Interpersonal Consequences

Consequential thinking can be practiced with games similar to the ones you used in the last chapter to practice thinking about alternative solutions. The word *might* is emphasized as it was in earlier ICPS word games because no one can predict what *will* happen next—consequences when other people are involved are never a certainty. Karena chose to begin this final ICPS step one Saturday afternoon when Tanya, Alison, and Alex were hanging around the kitchen complaining they had nothing to do.

With paper and pencil in hand, she said, "All right, come over here to the table and let's see if we can help a little boy I know solve his problem." Knowing this meant an ICPS game, the children ran to the table.

MOM: This boy, named Joey, wanted to feed the classroom hamster, but a girl named Jill was already standing by the cage getting ready to give the hamster his food. How can Joey get a chance to feed the hamster?

ALISON: I know! He could ask her if they could each give the hamster some.

MOM: That's one way. Remember, the idea of this game is to think of more than one way. Tanya, can you think of a DIFFERENT way?

TANYA: He could ask the teacher for a turn.

MOM: Good, you thought of a DIFFERENT way. Alex, can you think of a third way that Joey could get a chance to feed the hamster?

ALEX: He could just push the girl away.

MOM: Okay, let's think about that solution and make up a different kind of story, a story about what MIGHT happen next. Pretend the boy does push the girl away. That's something he can *do;* I'm going to write that solution here on the left side of my paper. *(Draws a line down the middle of the paper and writes in Alex's response on the left side.)*

He could push her.

MOM: Now listen carefully. This is a new question. IF the boy pushes the girl, what MIGHT happen next in the story?

ALISON: She might push him back.

MOM: Okay. The girl MIGHT push him back. I'm going to write all the things that MIGHT happen over here on the right side of this line. *(Writes down Alison's response.)* Now, let's think of lots of things that MIGHT happen next IF the boy pushes her away.

TANYA: She might cry.

MOM: Okay. The girl MIGHT cry. *(Writes down this possible consequence on the right side of the line and draws a line from the solution to the two consequences given thus far.)*

He could push her away. ⟨— She MIGHT push him back.
                          ⟨— She MIGHT cry.

MOM: IF the boy pushes the girl *(pointing to the left side of the paper)*, she MIGHT push him back *(dramatically darkening the arrow)* OR she might cry *(emphasizing the arrow again)*. OR what else MIGHT this girl do IF this boy pushes her away?

ALEX: She might tell her mother.

MOM: *(adds Alex's response to the list on the right side of her paper)* What MIGHT the girl say to the boy IF he pushes her?

TANYA: She might say, "Get out of here."

MOM: *(adds Tanya's response to the list on the right side of her paper)* Okay. How MIGHT the girl feel IF the boy pushes her away?

ALEX: Mad!

MOM: She MIGHT feel ANGRY IF the boy pushes her away *(adding this to the list)*. Look at all the things that MIGHT happen IF the boy uses Alex's solution to the problem *(reading down the right side of the paper):*

He could push
her away.

She MIGHT push him back.
She MIGHT cry.
She MIGHT tell her mother.
She MIGHT say, "Get out of here."
She MIGHT feel mad or ANGRY.

MOM: You all did a good job of thinking of DIFFERENT things that MIGHT happen next. We'll play this again later with a different problem, but right now let's have a snack.

The bored feeling was gone and the kids clambered around Karena for their snack. This introduction to considering consequences was short but successful.

The Process of Considering Consequences

As you can see from Karena's pretend-problem game, eliciting consequences is simply a matter of identifying the problem, thinking of a solution, and then asking, "What MIGHT happen next?" Writing down the children's responses and drawing arrows from the solution to the consequences helps them visualize (even if they can't read) that one action leads to another.

Like Karena, you'll find it helpful to follow these simple steps when you begin considering consequences with your children:

1. State the problem or have the child state the problem.
2. Elicit alternative solutions in the usual way.
3. Stop at a solution that is conducive to asking for consequences. (Usually, "hit," "grab," or "tell someone" are good ones to start with.)
4. Write this solution on the left side of your paper.
5. Announce that you're going to make up a *different* kind of story about what *might* happen next. Ask for lots of *different* responses.
6. List each response on the right side of your paper, drawing a line from the solution to each response.

Go ahead and let your kids try some consequential thinking. You might start out with a problem like this: Kyle had crayons and Tara had markers. Kyle wanted to use Tara's markers. What can he do to get to use the markers? Then ask for lots of different things that might happen if he does that.

(Notice that the question above includes the phrase "to use." If you ask, "What can you do *to get* the markers?" you're almost suggesting a response such as, "Take it.")

Helpful Hints

Hint No. 1: Keeping Consequences Coming

You can keep consequences coming in the same way you encouraged more solutions—without implying that the first response was "wrong." You'll want your children to know that you're asking them to think of more consequences because it's fun to think of lots of different things that might happen—not because you didn't like their first suggestion. So when you begin asking for different consequences, say, "That's *one* thing that MIGHT happen. Now, the idea of this game is to think of lots of things that MIGHT happen next IF . . ."

Hint No. 2: Eliciting Still More Consequences

If your children run out of responses to your question "What MIGHT happen next?" ask them, "What MIGHT _____ say?" or even "What MIGHT _____ do?"

Hint No. 3: Handling Chain Reactions

You want to talk only about direct consequences, not chain reactions. For instance, if Jon pushes Patricia, a direct consequence is that Patricia might push him back. When you ask for another consequence, your child may say, "Then Jon MIGHT throw a block at her." But Jon's throwing the block isn't the direct consequence of his first act of pushing Patricia—it's a chain reaction to being pushed back by Patricia.

If your child offers a chain reaction consequence, point it out and then get back on the right track. You could say, for example, "That MIGHT happen IF Jon gets pushed back by Patricia. But remember, we're thinking of lots of things that MIGHT happen next when Jon first pushes Patricia. Number one was that Patricia MIGHT push him back; what else MIGHT happen?"

Hint No. 4: Handling Unclear or Seemingly Irrelevant Responses

Handle unclear or seemingly irrelevant responses in the same way you handled them when you were thinking of alternative solutions. First, find out what the child has in mind; it's especially important to question the child as to who is doing the action. For example, in the problem about the boy who wanted to feed the hamster, the response "grab the food" could either be a solution enacted by the boy or a consequence enacted by the girl. In this case you would ask your child to explain who grabbed the food. And if the child says the boy grabbed the food (which is a solution for the boy), you can follow with: "That's what the *boy* could do to get to feed the hamster. Remember, we're talking about what the *girl* MIGHT say OR *do* IF the boy pushes her away."

Hint No. 5: Responding to "Nothing Will Happen" or "I Don't Know" Responses

When you ask your children, "What MIGHT happen next?" they may respond, "Nothing," or "I don't know." Either may be a genuine response that shows they're stuck and can't think of anything, but either can also mean they don't care, don't want to think about it, or simply don't want to play the game anymore. If this happens, try to figure out if it's an "I'm stuck" or an "I don't care" response. If your children aren't interested in playing ICPS at that moment, take a break. There're always plenty more opportunities to use ICPS later. If your children feel stuck and can't think of an answer, you can encourage consequential thinking by continuing the dialogue.

If your children respond to your question "What MIGHT happen next?" with "Nothing," you can say, "MAYBE nothing will happen, but let's just make up something that MIGHT happen." Encourage your children to "pretend" a consequence.

If your children say, "I don't know," agree with them that no one can be sure what will happen, but then encourage them to play the game by pretending and making up something that *might* happen.

Hint No. 6: Handling Enumerations

As you saw when you began asking for alternative solutions, some children will give variations on a theme that aren't really *different* responses. If this happens when you're asking for consequences, point out that those things are "kind of the same BECAUSE they're ALL _____ (e.g., telling someone)." Then ask for something that *might* happen that is *different*.

Similar to enumerations used in solution finding, examples of enumerations your kids might offer when considering consequences include:

tell her mother/tell her father/tell her teacher (all telling someone)

hit/punch/slap (all hurting someone)

scream/yell/holler (all showing anger with your voice)

Solutions and Consequences

Once your children seem to understand the idea that solutions have consequences, you can use a shorter version of the solution-consequence game by combining alternative solution finding with consequential thinking.

Let's say you present this problem to your children:

Betty has a toy that Derek wants to play with. How can Derek get the toy?

First ask your children to think of one solution:

Solution: He could ask for it.

Then ask for one possible consequence:

Consequence: She'll give it to him.

Continue to ask for solution-consequence pairs as long as time and interest allow. Some possible pairs for this example might include:

1. He could kick her. ⟶ She'll cry.
2. He could say, "I won't ⟶ She won't care.
   be your friend."
3. He could ask for it. ⟶ She'll give it to him.
4. He could offer to trade ⟶ She'll trade.
   it for his crayons.
5. He could grab it. ⟶ She'll grab it back.

When introduced as a game, this kind of thinking process becomes a playful, fun activity for children. Then later, you'll find that when your children have a real-life problem to solve, they'll be willing and even eager to consider your suggestion "You have a problem; let's think of solutions AND their consequences," or even still shorter, as Alison was heard telling Alex one day, "Let's ICPS this."

Puppet Play

As always, puppets are a fun way to help children practice new ICPS skills. One day shortly after Karena introduced the boy and the hamster problem, she stayed home from work to be with Tanya, who was sick with a sore throat and earache. Knowing that Tanya always enjoyed puppet play, Karena brought out Ollie and Tippy to help her pass the time and to give her more practice at thinking of solutions and consequences. Their little play went something like this:

MOM: Oh, dear. Ollie and Tippy have a problem and they need some help solving it.

TIPPY: Ollie is using my paints.

OLLIE: No, I'm NOT. These are *my* paints.

MOM: Tanya, do Tippy and Ollie see the problem the SAME way OR a DIFFERENT way?

TANYA: A different way.

MOM: That means we have a problem to solve. How are you feeling, Tippy?

TIPPY: ANGRY. I'm going to hit Ollie right in the face if he doesn't give me back my paints.

MOM: Tanya, what MIGHT happen IF Tippy hits Ollie in the face?

TANYA: I think he will tell his mother.

MOM: That's one thing that MIGHT happen. What else MIGHT happen?

TANYA: He might cry.

MOM: *(looking to clarify what could be an irrelevant response)* Who MIGHT cry?

TANYA: Ollie.

MOM: Ollie MIGHT cry IF Tippy hits him. What else MIGHT happen?

TANYA: He might hit Tippy back.

MOM: That's another thing that MIGHT happen. What is another way Tippy can get Ollie to give her back her paints so Ollie won't cry or hit back?

TANYA: Maybe he could ask to trade some paints for some other toy.

MOM: What MIGHT happen IF he does that?

TANYA: Ollie MIGHT say "okay" and give Tippy some paints.

In this puppet play, Karena began to push the idea of considering consequences a bit further. She asked her daughter to consider another solution when the consequences of the first one seemed undesirable. This is the ultimate goal of ICPS problem solving—to *evaluate* the consequences and decide if the solution *is* or *is not* a good one.

Evaluating Solutions

Alison and Alex told their mom all about the hamster problem they had talked about at Tanya's house. So a few days later Marie went back to the hamster problem to continue practicing the idea that solutions have consequences. She also wanted to add the idea that some consequences make a solution a good one, and some consequences make a solution a not-so-good one. When children understand this, they're able to judge for themselves when they should act on a solution they've thought of. Also they'll know from their solution-finding games that when they think a solution won't really solve the problem, they can always think of a different way. That's what I mean when I say that ICPS teaches kids *how*, not *what*, to think so that in time they will be able to solve real-life problems successfully.

Marie began, "Remember the story about the boy who wanted to feed the hamster and so he decided to push the girl out of the way? Remember you thought that IF the boy pushed her, she MIGHT push him back, cry, OR tell her mother? Let me ask each of you a question: Alison, IF pushing the girl causes these things to happen, do you think the solution 'push her' IS a good one?"

"No," said Alison.

"Why not?" continued her mom.

" 'CAUSE it just isn't."

Looking for a more exact reason, Mom asked, "How do you think being pushed would make the girl feel?"

"Probably sad or angry."

"Is pushing a good idea or not a good idea?"

"NOT a good idea."

"Alex," asked Mom, "what do you think? IF pushing MIGHT cause the girl to push back, cry, OR tell her mother, is it a good idea or not a good idea?"

"Not a good idea," agreed Alex.

"Well then, if pushing the girl IS NOT a good solution, what DIFFERENT idea can the boy think of so he can feed the hamster?"

"Maybe he could just ask her," suggested Alex.

"I'm going to write that down," said Mom. "Now, let's think about what MIGHT happen next IF he asks her. Alison, what MIGHT happen next?"

"She might say yes."

"But," yelled Alex, "she MIGHT say no!"

"Okay," said Mom, writing down this consequence on the paper. "I'm writing down, 'She MIGHT say yes or she MIGHT say no.' Now, Alex, can you think of something DIFFERENT that MIGHT happen IF he asks the girl?"

"She might say they can share the food."

"All right, let's write that down."

He could ask. ⟨— She MIGHT say yes (or no).
⟨— She MIGHT let him share.

Now," said Mom, pointing to her paper, "IF he asks the girl, she MIGHT say yes, she MIGHT say no, OR she MIGHT offer to share the hamster food. Alex, do you think asking the girl IS a good solution?"

"Yeah."

"WHY? Does this solve the boy's problem?" asked Mom.

"Yeah, if she says yes."

"What can the boy do IF she says no?" asked Mom.

"I know!" jumped in Alison. "He can think of a DIFFER-ENT way."

"Yes, he can," answered Mom. "When the first way turns out to be a not-so-good way, you can always try another way."

Evaluating solutions by considering consequences is an especially important skill for impulsive problem solvers like Alex. His usual way is to think of a solution to a problem and jump on it. Practicing this skill of thinking *before* doing anything will greatly improve the way he interacts with other people.

Hint No. 7: Handling Undesirable Solutions

When you give kids the freedom to think of ways to solve their own problems, once in a while they'll come up with solutions you may not like—like pushing the girl away from the hamster cage, which at first seemed like a perfectly good solution to Alex. But don't worry; research shows that when kids learn to think the ICPS way, they are, in time, less likely to *act* on the kinds of solutions that don't really solve the problem. Still, Marie was able to help Alex think of a solution with a less negative impact on others by expanding the dialogue to make him think a bit more about the consequences of his solution.

In the same way, your children might decide that grabbing a toy away from a friend is a good solution because "I'll get what I want." If your children offer solutions that seem inappropriate or undesirable, you can get them to reevaluate their ideas by asking questions such as:

"How would _____ feel IF you did that?"

"What else MIGHT happen IF you do that?"

"How would you feel IF that happened?"

"What is something DIFFERENT you can do so that won't happen?"

Daily Use in Problem Situations

ICPS games and activities help children understand that different solutions have different consequences. This prepares them for real-life circumstances in which they find out firsthand if a solution they've decided on will really solve the problem.

Let's say, for example, your child tells you that she thinks she can get her friend to play hopscotch if, in exchange, she offers to ride bicycles later. If after you guide her to consider the consequence of this solution, she decides it is a good one, tell her: "Go ahead and try that."

If the solution works, say, "Oh, you thought of that all by yourself. You're a good problem solver!"

If the solution does not work, say, "You'll have to think of something DIFFERENT. I know you're a good thinker!"

If your child offers a negative solution such as some form of a threat, you might ask the child, "What MIGHT happen?" and "How MIGHT people feel?" and then help him or her to see that there's more than one way.

Take a look at how Marie used a full dialogue to help Alison solve her problem with Alex:

MOM: Why did you grab that crayon from Alex?
ALISON: Because he never shares.
     (This identifies the problem.)

MOM: How do you think Alex feels when you grab the crayon away from him?
> *(Alison is asked to consider Alex's feelings.)*

ALISON: ANGRY.
MOM: What MIGHT happen next?
> *(Alison is asked to consider the consequences of her act.)*

ALISON: He'll hit me.
MOM: How would you feel if that happened?
> *(Alison considers her own feelings too.)*

ALISON: SAD and ANGRY.
MOM: Grabbing is *one* thing you can do to get the crayon. Can you think of something DIFFERENT you can do so Alex won't be ANGRY and you won't be SAD?
ALISON: I can ask him.
> *(Alison thinks of her own alternative solution.)*

MOM: That's a DIFFERENT idea. What do you think MIGHT happen IF you ask him?
> *(Alison is asked to anticipate consequences to the solution.)*

ALISON: He might say yes.
MOM: Go ahead and try that.
ALISON: Can I have the blue crayon?
ALEX: No!
MOM: That way didn't work. Can you think of a second DIFFERENT way?
ALISON: I could say, "I'll let you use my markers."
> *(Alison thinks of a DIFFERENT alternative solution.)*

MOM: What do think MIGHT happen IF you do that?

*(Alison is asked to anticipate
consequences to this solution, too.)*

ALISON: This time I think he'll share.
MOM: Give it a try.
ALISON: Alex, if you let me use the blue crayon, I'll let you use
my markers.
ALEX: Okay.
MOM: You thought of that all by yourself. You're a good prob-
lem solver.

Cutting It Short

This dialogue took no longer than the time it would have
taken Marie to scold Alison for grabbing, instruct Alex to
share, and then mediate the arguments that surely would have
followed. Still, after your children develop the habit of thinking about others' feelings and alternative solutions and consequences, you can usually shorten your ICPS dialogues. Because
Alison is generally a good problem solver, Marie probably
could have helped Alison solve her problem in the example
above by simply asking, "Can you think of a DIFFERENT way
to solve your problem?"

Even more impulsive problem solvers like Alex will respond
to shorter ICPS dialogues after they've spent enough time
practicing the thinking skills to understand the total concept.
One day when Alex wanted his mother to let him play a video
game just before dinner, Mom avoided a tantrum by asking,
"How will you feel at dinnertime when I have to stop you in
the middle of your game?"

"FRRUSSS . . . TRATED," said Alex, proudly pronouncing
his new, big word.

Then Mom asked, "Can you think of something DIFFER-

ENT to do NOW so you won't have to stop in the middle?"
After thinking a minute—a big step for Alex—he said, "I'll
play ball outside." In this instance, a short ICPS dialogue
worked just fine.

Growing with ICPS

In addition to the benefits you'll find in using ICPS dialogues to help your children think about real-life problem
situations, you may also notice an overall change in your children's behavior as they continue practicing these thinking
skills. Tanya, Alex, and Alison all grew in remarkable ways
after learning ICPS.

Tanya, for example, not only grew more confident and vo-
cal when playing ICPS games, she also learned how to com-
municate better with other children. ICPS didn't completely
change Tanya's shyness, but she was no longer timid and
fearful of other children; it helped her deal with her feelings
and relate to others. In Chapter Five, when Tanya wanted to
play jump rope with the other girls, she was able to think of
a different way to get what she wanted ("If you need somebody to hold the rope, I could do it"). This was a major
breakthrough in the way Tanya acted with other children. At
another time, Tanya's mom watched as a child jumped on
the playground swing just as Tanya was about to sit on it.
Before ICPS, Tanya would have walked away feeling hurt
and frustrated; she might even have run crying to her
mother. But this time Tanya thought of a different way to
react. She stood next to the swing and said, "AFTER you
finish, then it will be my turn."

Shy children who haven't learned ICPS skills turn away
from confrontational situations because they don't know what
to say or how to respond with confidence. But Tanya is now

able to speak up, giving clear evidence that ICPS is influencing how she responds to problem situations.

Alex, too, showed very impressive growth in the way he acted toward others. Very notably, he seemed much more sensitive to his younger brother's feelings. In one instance in particular, Marie entered the room to find Peter crying and Alex holding Peter's blanket. "What's happening here?" she asked.

"Alex took Peter's blanket," said Alison.

"But let me tell you WHY," pleaded Alex.

"This way of responding," Marie later told me, "took me by surprise. Alex knew it was important for me to know what the real problem was. I thought he took the blanket to make Peter cry like he often does, but it turned out that Alex wanted to use the blanket to make a little tent for Peter."

"I thought that would make him feel HAPPY," Alex told his mom.

"I'm so glad ICPS taught me not to rush in and start scolding Alex for taking things from his brother. My little troublemaker was trying to do something nice, and ICPS helped both of us understand that." Rather than punish Alex, Marie helped him understand that Peter cried because Alex took his blanket and then helped him think of a way to build a tent without first upsetting his brother.

Even with his friends, Alex was finding *different,* less aggressive ways to solve his problems. One day at preschool, for example, Alex wanted Richard to get out of the wagon because "It's my turn now." When Richard said, "I'm playing with it," Alex did not create a new problem by hitting or kicking him. Instead, he thought of a *different* way. "If you let me have the wagon," he said, "I'll give it right back."

Richard didn't answer.

Alex then asked, "Why can't I have it?"

"Because," Richard replied, "I need it. I'm pulling the rocks."

"I'll pull them with you, okay?" shouted Alex.

"Okay," said Richard. And the two boys played with the wagon together.

Surely Alex's days of hitting and kicking are not completely behind him; it takes quite a while for a pattern of thinking to become an automatic response. But for now, as Alex is finishing the "lessons" of ICPS, he is already showing impressive signs of growth. Now that he is beginning to learn about alternative possible solutions and appreciate their consequences, he is more able to solve his problems effectively. This ability helps him to feel frustrated less frequently and to get along better with his family and friends.

Even Alison, who by nature is a good problem solver, benefited from ICPS. The ICPS process of thinking about problems enhanced and reinforced her natural abilities. It's also possible that increasing these skills in children like Alison can prevent later problems because this style of thinking is perpetuated. This process also helped keep Alison on the ICPS track by giving her natural thinking skills family acceptance and support.

Putting It All Together

There are no more steps to add to ICPS. You now have all you need to use full ICPS dialogues to help your children solve their problems.

Pulled all together, a full ICPS dialogue has four parts; it helps children:

1. identify the problem;
2. appreciate how they and others feel;

3. think of solutions to solve the problem; and
4. anticipate consequences of the solutions.

Take a look back at Chapter One. Marie began ICPS feeling perhaps as you did, unsure of what was expected of her and a bit uncomfortable about rethinking her natural inclination to *tell* her children what to do—"Stop grabbing!"—or even explain "Because you might lose a friend." As an overview at that introductory point, I included a full sample dialogue to illustrate how Marie would later learn to help Alex think about his toy-grabbing problem. Becoming a full-fledged ICPS mom took time for Marie. And, at first, the dialogue may have looked rather long and structured to you. But now, as we've come full circle and look back, you can see that the dialogue simply followed the four steps listed above:

MOM: Alex, your teacher tells me you're grabbing toys again. Tell me what happened.
(Mom helps child identify the problem.)

ALEX: Jonathan had my magnets. He wouldn't give them back.
MOM: Why did you have to have them back right then?
ALEX: 'Cause he had a long turn.
MOM: How do you think Jonathan feels when you grab toys like that?
*(Mom helps child think about
the other child's feelings.)*

ALEX: Mad, but I don't care; they're mine.
MOM: What did Jonathan do when you grabbed the toy?
*(Mom helps child think about the
consequences of his act.)*

ALEX: He hit me.
MOM: How did that make you feel?
(Mom helps child think about his feelings, too.)

ALEX: Mad.

MOM: You're ANGRY AND your friend IS ANGRY, and he hit you. Can you think of a DIFFERENT way to get your toy back so you both won't be ANGRY and so Jonathan will not hit you?

ALEX: I could ask him.

MOM: And what MIGHT happen then?
> *(Mom guides child to think of consequences
> to positive solutions, too.)*

ALEX: He'll say no.

MOM: He MIGHT say no. What else can you think of doing to get your toy back?
> *(Staying focused on the child's problem, Mom
> encourages him to think of more solutions.)*

ALEX: I could let him play with my toy cars.

MOM: Good thinking. You thought of two DIFFERENT ways.

This "long" dialogue illustrates each step of ICPS thinking yet takes less than a minute to deliver—but it can be shortened and still be effective. After Alex became familiar with the four steps of ICPS dialogues, his mom was able to use shorter versions to prompt him to redirect his way of thinking about a problem. For the grabbing problem, she might simply say: "Alex, can you think of a DIFFERENT way to get your toys back so you won't both be ANGRY and Jonathan won't hit you?" All by itself, this kind of question is often enough to guide Alex to think of feelings, alternative solutions, and consequences.

In either case, long or short, Alex's mother didn't try to solve the problem the "right" way from her point of view. She didn't tell her son to share or even explain why he shouldn't grab. Her questions helped Alex think about the problem, his own and others' feelings, the consequences of what he does, and what else he can do. That's ICPS thinking.

Like Alex, your children now have the skills they need to think about any problem they come up against in dealing with other people. With ICPS they haven't been told *what* to think, but they do know *how* to think—and when faced with problems throughout their lives, that's what really matters.

◆ ◆ ◆

When you have finished the games, and the activities, and the puppet plays detailed in Part I, the ICPS door to a happier and more socially fulfilling life has been opened, but don't let your kids stop at the doorway. Now it's time to build the *habit* of using these skills. Each day, with each new problem, remember ICPS. You can use ICPS when you talk about problems in story books, on TV, in the news, in your neighborhood, and certainly in your home. ICPS can become a way of thinking that will be useful to your children throughout their lives.

Part II of this book is included as a resource for your continued use of ICPS in the years to come. It lists, in an easy reference form, games and activities that support Interpersonal Cognitive Problem Solving (ICPS) skills; it then offers sample dialogues that will help you quickly refresh your memory without having to reread whole chapters.

PART II

Putting the Pieces Together

7

◆ ● ◆

ICPS Games and Activities

Throughout Part I of this book, you've looked on as Alex, Alison, and Tanya played lots of ICPS games and activities. You've probably used their example as a springboard from which to teach your own children the skills of ICPS. But, as when learning any new skill, going through the process once is just the beginning. Skills need to be practiced over and over before they can be used proficiently and without prompting.

The following games are listed here to give you more ideas for practicing ICPS. They suggest ways of talking with your children that reinforce their understanding of the words and feelings involved in problem solving. They'll remind you that when you sit down to eat, or get into your car to run errands, or even when you help with homework, you have an opportunity to practice ICPS thinking skills.

But remember, these are only suggestions. They are but a few of the many ways you can play ICPS word games. In fact, because ICPS moments pop up so often during the day, you may want to keep your own ICPS notebook where you can jot down ideas and record moments when an ICPS activity worked especially well for you. That will make a handy reference source through the years as you occasionally return to this chapter for an ICPS refresher.

In whatever games you play, remember to use only the concepts your child knows. If your four-year-old, for example, still can't distinguish between the feelings of *proud* and *frustrated,* then don't use these words in your games. You can use my suggestions to match your at-home activities to your child's level.

Playing with Words at Any Time

Is/Is Not

"_____ IS a basketball (baseball, etc.) player. He is NOT a _____ player."

"Today IS Tuesday. It is NOT _____."

Or/And

"Today the weather is hot AND _____."

"You can color your picture with markers OR with _____."

Some/All

"Are SOME of my children in the room or ALL of my children?"

"Did you pick up SOME of your toys or ALL of your toys?"

Same/Different

"Does this penny look the SAME as this nickel or DIFFERENT?"

"Do you like to eat the SAME foods as your friend or DIFFERENT foods?"

Might/Maybe

"You should bring an umbrella if you think it MIGHT _____."

Before/After

"Were you born BEFORE or AFTER Grandma was born?"

"Should you put on your shoes BEFORE or AFTER your socks?"

If/Then

"IF we are sitting, THEN we are NOT _____."

"IF you are playing with clay, THEN you are NOT _____."

Why/Because

"This is a good day to go swimming. Can you guess WHY it's a good day to go swimming?"

"Can you finish this sentence? I should wear my coat today BECAUSE _____."

Fair/Not Fair

"Did anything happen in school today that was NOT FAIR?"

Considering Feelings

"What makes your mom (dad, brother, sister, etc.) feel HAPPY? SAD? ANGRY? PROUD? FRUSTRATED?"

"What do you do that makes your mom (dad, brother, sister, etc.) feel HAPPY? ANGRY? PROUD? FRUSTRATED?"

"Name the last time you felt HAPPY, SAD, ANGRY, PROUD, FRUSTRATED."

"When you finish this project, will you feel HAPPY? SAD? ANGRY? PROUD? FRUSTRATED?"

"How do you feel when your team wins the game?"

"Did anything happen to you today that made you feel HAPPY? SAD? ANGRY? PROUD? FRUSTRATED?"

"How can you tell if your pet feels HAPPY? SAD? ANGRY?"

"Tying a shoelace can be very difficult. Do you feel HAPPY or FRUSTRATED when you can't get it tied?"

Playing with Words at Bedtime

Is/Is Not

"It IS time to go to bed. It is NOT time to _____."

Or/And

"When you go to bed, do you want the door open OR closed?"

"When you go into bed, shut off the light AND open (close) your door."

Some/All

"Do you want to sleep with SOME of your dolls or ALL of them?"

Before/After

"Do you brush your teeth BEFORE or AFTER you go to bed?"

If/Then/Might

"IF you go to bed, late THEN what MIGHT happen in the morning?"

"IF you don't put the blanket on, THEN what MIGHT happen?"

Now/Later

"What MIGHT happen IF you do NOT go to bed NOW?"

"Is it a good idea to go to bed NOW or LATER?"

Why/Because

"Do you know WHY we have to sleep each night?"

Fair/Not Fair

"WHY do you think it's NOT FAIR that your brother can go to bed later than you?"

Considering Feelings

"How do you feel when it's time for bed?"

"How do you feel when it's time to wake up in the morning?"

Playing with Words at Homework Time

You can often use ICPS words when you talk to your children about their homework assignments. In addition, in the early primary grades, children often bring home papers that show their classwork with letters, colors, and shapes. When you go over these papers with your children, you can reinforce the lesson using ICPS vocabulary words. The following will give you a few ideas on how to relate classwork to ICPS.

Is/Is Not

"This IS the letter *A*. It is NOT the letter (*child responds*)."

"This IS a circle. It is NOT a (*child responds*)."

Or/And

"Is this the letter *A* OR the letter *B*?"

"Is this your spelling homework OR your math homework?"

"You have two kinds of homework tonight. You have reading homework AND _____ homework."

Some/All

"Show me ALL of the circles."

"Point to SOME but not ALL of the squares on this page."

Same/Different

"Show me two circles that are DIFFERENT colors."

"Show me two circles that are the SAME color AND one circle that is a DIFFERENT color."

Before/After

"Does the letter *B* come BEFORE or AFTER the letter *C*?"

"Does the number 5 come BEFORE or AFTER the number 2?"

If/Then/Might

"IF you do a good job on your homework, THEN what MIGHT happen in school tomorrow?"

"IF you study your spelling words, THEN how MIGHT you do on your test?"

Why/Because

"Homework is important BECAUSE _____."

"WHY do you think your teacher asks you to do homework?"

Fair/Not Fair

"Would it be FAIR for you to copy your homework from your friend?"

Considering Feelings

"How does homework make you feel?"

"If you don't do this homework, how do you think you'll feel in school tomorrow when the teacher asks to see it?"

"Your teacher put a star on this homework paper. How does that make you feel? (*If needed:* PROUD? or FRUSTRATED?)"

"I know you're trying to solve this math problem and you find it hard; how does that make you feel? (*If needed:* PROUD? or FRUSTRATED?)"

Playing with Words at Mealtime

Is/Is Not

"This IS pizza. It is NOT a _____."

Or/And

"Is this pizza OR an egg?"

"Pizza is made of dough, cheese, AND _____."

Some/All

"Did you eat SOME of your pizza or ALL of it?"

Same/Different

"Show me something that is the SAME color as your pizza."

"Show me something on the table that is a DIFFERENT shape than your pizza."

Might/Maybe

"What MIGHT happen IF you eat ALL the pizza by yourself?"

Before/After

"Do we eat pizza BEFORE or AFTER we go to bed?"

Now/Later

"Do you want more pizza NOW or LATER?"

If/Then

"IF this IS pizza, THEN it is NOT _____."

"IF you put soda in your cup, THEN you can NOT put _____ in the cup."

Why/Because

"You can't eat the whole pizza BECAUSE _____."

"We can't eat pizza every night BECAUSE _____."

Fair/Not Fair

"Would it be FAIR or NOT FAIR if I ate two pieces and gave you only one piece?"

"Would it be FAIR to eat ALL the pizza without saving any for Dad?"

Considering Feelings

"Would you feel HAPPY if you had a big piece of pizza OR a little piece of pizza?"

"Who would NOT feel HAPPY with a big piece of pizza?"

"Do ALL of us feel the SAME way about pizza, OR do SOME of us feel a DIFFERENT way?"

Playing with Words While Grocery Shopping

Is/Is Not

"This IS a food store. It is NOT a _____ store."

"Show me a fruit that IS red."

"Show me a vegetable that is NOT a carrot."

Or/And

"Would you like me to buy cookies OR crackers?"

"To make a peanut butter and jelly sandwich, I need to buy peanut butter, jelly, AND _____."

Same/Different

"Watermelon and honeydew are both melons. Do they look the SAME or DIFFERENT?"

"Do you want me to buy the SAME kind of cereal we bought last time or a DIFFERENT kind?"

(You can give your child a coupon with a picture of a food item. Standing in that particular food section, ask the following): "Show me the food that looks the SAME as the one in the picture."

Some/All

"Are ALL of these melons the SAME size or are SOME of them DIFFERENT?"

Before/After

"Do we pay for our food BEFORE or AFTER we take it off the shelf?"

"Do you know where this corn came from BEFORE it came to this store?"

Now/Later

"Should we open this package of noodles NOW or wait until LATER?"

"What MIGHT happen IF we open it NOW?"

If/Then

"IF we don't go food shopping, THEN what MIGHT happen?"

"IF I buy only snacks and no real food for dinner, THEN what MIGHT happen?"

Why/Because

"Do you know WHY the ice cream is kept in a refrigerator?"

"I'm putting the apples in a plastic bag BECAUSE _____."

Fair/Not Fair

"Would it be FAIR to buy you a special treat and not buy one for your brother?"

Considering Feelings

"Is there any food that makes you feel HAPPY?"

"Is there any food that makes you feel a DIFFERENT way?"

"When the farmer picked these beautiful peaches off the tree, do you think he felt PROUD or FRUSTRATED?"

Playing with Words at Story Time

You can play many word games by pointing to the pictures in a storybook and asking questions such as the following, which refer to the classic story "Little Red Riding Hood."

Is/Is Not

"This IS a girl. She is NOT a _____."

"The girl IS wearing a red coat. She is NOT wearing _____."

Some/All

"Are ALL the children in the story girls, or are SOME of them boys?"

Same/Different

"Did Little Red Riding Hood's grandmother look the SAME or DIFFERENT when Little Red Riding Hood arrived at her house?"

Might/Maybe

"What MIGHT happen next?"

Before/After

"Did the wolf eat Grandma BEFORE or AFTER Little Red Riding Hood arrived?"

Now/Later

"Do you want to finish this story NOW or LATER?"

If/Then

"IF Little Red Riding Hood had listened to her mother, THEN what MIGHT have happened?"

"IF Little Red Riding Hood did not talk to the wolf in the woods, THEN what might NOT have happened?"

Why/Because

"Little Red Riding Hood was surprised when she saw her grandmother BECAUSE _____."

"Do you know WHY Little Red Riding Hood should NOT have talked to the wolf?"

Fair/Not Fair

"Do you think it was FAIR for the wolf to trick Little Red Riding Hood?"

Considering Feelings

When reading a storybook to your child, stop at appropriate places and ask questions such as the following.

"How do you think this character felt when _____ *(describe the event)*?"

"WHY do you think he/she felt that way?"

"Would you feel the SAME way OR a DIFFERENT way?"

"WHY would you feel that way?"

"What new, DIFFERENT things would also make you feel that way?"

"How could another person in the story help the girl feel HAPPY again?"

Thinking About Solutions and Consequences

Because stories involve personal conflicts, they can be used to practice thinking about solutions and consequences. You can use ICPS thinking skills during your story time by stopping occasionally and asking questions such as the following.

"Do you think that the girl used a good solution to solve her problem? WHY or WHY NOT?"

"Can you think of a DIFFERENT way the girl MIGHT have solved that problem?"

"What MIGHT have happened IF she used your solution?"

"How else MIGHT the story have ended?"

Playing with Words at Travel Time

Is/Is Not

"We are riding in the car. We are NOT riding _____."

"When you're traveling in a car, you can look out the window but you can NOT _____."

Or/And

"You can sit in the front seat OR you can sit in the back."

"When you get into the car, you should do two things: close the door AND _____ *(put on your seat belt).*"

Some/All

"Do you think we should put SOME of the packages in the trunk or ALL of them?"

"Can we fit ALL your friends in our car or only SOME of them?"

"Do you like to ride the bus ALL of the time or SOME of the time?"

Same/Different

"Does your friend have the SAME kind of car as we do or a DIFFERENT kind of car?"

"Is the inside of the car the SAME color as the outside or a DIFFERENT color?"

"Does our car look the SAME as a bus or DIFFERENT?"

Before/After

"Should you put your seat belt on BEFORE or AFTER I start driving?"

Now/Later

"I'm very low on gas. Do you think I should fill up NOW or LATER?"

"Do you want to stop for lunch NOW or LATER?"

If/Then/Might

"IF you don't wear your seat belt, THEN what MIGHT happen?"

"IF you stick your arm out the window, THEN what MIGHT happen?"

Why/Because

"Do you know WHY I can't drive ahead when the light turns red?"

"Do you know WHY cars need gas?"

Fair/Not Fair

"You sat in the front seat of the car the last time. Is it FAIR for your sister to sit in the backseat again?"

Considering Feelings

"Are you HAPPIER when you walk to school or when you get a ride?"

"How do you feel when the bus is late?"

Playing with Words at TV Time

Is/Is Not

"We ARE watching cartoons. We are NOT watching _____."

"Do you think what he did IS or is NOT a good idea?"

Or/And

"Do you want to watch *(name of show)* OR *(name of another show)*?"

Some/All

"Are ALL of the characters on this show funny or only SOME of them?"

"Do ALL of your friends watch this show or SOME of them?"

Same/Different

"You can't watch *(name of show)* AND *(name of another show)* at the SAME time."

"Do those two characters see the problem in the SAME or a DIFFERENT way?"

Might/Maybe

"What do you think MIGHT happen next?"

Before/After

"Should I turn off the TV BEFORE or AFTER this show is over?"

"Do you want a snack BEFORE or AFTER the commercial?"

If/Then/Now/Later

"IF you watch TV NOW, THEN you can NOT watch it
_____ (*if needed:* NOW? or LATER?))."

Why/Because

"Do you know WHY that character is laughing?"

"Can you finish this sentence? That man is cleaning the
house BECAUSE _____."

Fair/Not Fair

"Do you think that what just happened on that show was
FAIR?"

"WHY do you think that?"

(If NOT FAIR): "What could have happened that would
have been FAIR?"

Considering Feelings

"How does that character feel?"

"WHY does he feel that way?"

"Would you feel the SAME way OR a DIFFERENT
way?"

Thinking About Solutions and Consequences

"What's the problem in this story?"

"The problem probably happened BECAUSE _____."

"How did the person feel when *(name event)*?"

"What did the character do or say to solve the problem?"

"Did anyone else try to solve the problem?"

"What happened AFTER the character tried to solve the problem?"

"Was the solution tried at a GOOD TIME or NOT A GOOD TIME?"

"Was the solution a good idea or NOT a good idea?"

"Can you think of a DIFFERENT way to solve this problem?"

Games and Activities About Problem Situations

You can easily weave the previously suggested activities into your daily schedule. But you can also use games to help your children continue thinking about problems and how to solve them. The following are a few ideas I've seen kids enjoy over the years. And remember, you can make up your own and even ask your kids to make up a few themselves.

The Memory Game

Kids love the memory game—it's fun, competitive, and a wonderful way to practice ICPS thinking. To play this game with your kids, you'll need to make two copies of each of the illustrations on pages 158 to 159 and then cut them into playing cards. As with commercial memory games (remember Concentration?), mix up the cards and place them face down. You're now ready to begin.

Ask your child to turn two cards face up. If the cards don't match, tell him to try to remember the pictures and their location and then turn them back face down. If the cards do match, your child can keep the cards *if* he can answer four questions about the picture:

1. "What's the problem?"
2. "How does the person in the picture feel about the problem?"
3. "What's a possible solution to the problem?"
4. "What MIGHT happen if the person in the picture really does (says) that?"

When all the cards are played, the player with the most matching sets wins the game.

There are several ways you can vary the rules of the memory game. You may decide that when a match is made, the child must think of two solutions and two consequences. Or you may want the child to state one solution with three possible consequences. Or you might even use the game to review only solution finding by asking the child to think of three possible solutions. Any way you want to play, you'll find this a very enjoyable way to practice the thinking skills of ICPS.

Puppet Stories

The puppet stories played in each chapter can be repeated and changed over and over again for hours of fun and learning. If your child has puppets, or dolls, or stuffed animals, or even just two socks, you've got all you need to practice ICPS.

Depending on your child's willingness and interest, either you can hold both puppets, or you and your child can each hold one. As your child becomes confident in ICPS skills, she may want to hold both puppets and put on a show to entertain you.

When you play, provide your puppets with a problem to solve. You might pretend, for example, that one puppet wants to go outside and play, but the other puppet wants to stay inside and play. Guide your child through the four parts of an ICPS dialogue by asking the puppets:

1. "What's the problem?"
2. "How do you feel about that?"
3. "How can you solve the problem?"
4. "What MIGHT happen if you try that?"

Stage Plays

Some children love to put on stage plays. They dress up and perform little skits for family and friends. If your children like this kind of thing, you can guide them to role-play problem situations. They might, for example, pretend that they are on the playground and one child won't go down the slide. Ask your children to think about what they can do or say to get a turn on the slide. Then let them act out the problem and their solutions.

Wall Pictures

Several children I've met have made a game out of the ICPS pictures scattered throughout this book. Their parents have made copies of the pictures and hung them on the wall. Then, every once in a while, the children make up new problem situations to match the pictures and tell a story about what's going on, how the problems might be solved, and what might happen if those solutions are used. This game is a nice way to remind your children visually to think about ICPS.

An ICPS Book (for Real Problems)

An ICPS Book is like a diary for young children. To begin an ICPS Book, get your children notepads of any kind in which they can draw pictures to record their problems and feelings. Encourage them, for example, to draw a face that shows how they feel about a certain problem. Ask them to draw a picture of themselves solving that problem, and then tell them to draw a face that shows how they will feel if the solution they choose solves the problem. If your children would like, they can also dictate problems and solutions to you. After you write the story in their ICPS Book, they can illustrate it. Later, your children will enjoy going back and listening to you read about their problems and how they were solved. These drawing, writing, and reading activities help children practice thinking about problems, feelings, solutions, and consequences.

8

◆ ● ◆

Sample ICPS Dialogues

This chapter is not a cookbook of precisely measured recipes for raising thinking children. I don't expect that you'll read and memorize every dialogue and I certainly don't want you to think that they represent the only way to use ICPS with your children in the given situations. ICPS dialoguing is a style of talk with children but it is not based on a memorized script.

The dialogues will be most useful to you if you use them as a handy reference guide. Let's say, for example, that you find yourself slipping back into old habits—you find that you can't stand the bickering and arguing that goes on among your children, and you revert to yelling. Rather than read through the whole book to get back on the ICPS track, a quick look through this chapter will remind you how you can talk about the problem the ICPS way. To make it even easier for you, if your child has a persistent problem that you seem to be losing ground on—let's say grabbing toys away from other children— you can look up Grabbing in this chapter (by checking the list on page 191) and refresh your memory about the questions you want to ask your child in this circumstance. The next time he grabs a toy, you'll be ready to ICPS immediately.

So this chapter can be used with a bookmark. If you need a quick refresher or have a specific problem you want to ICPS, here's where you can quickly brush up on the skill of raising an ICPS thinker.

Child-Child Problems

Child-child problems are ones that occur between children and their friends. As your children are learning and practicing ICPS, your role is to listen for when these kinds of problems occur and then to ask questions that prompt ICPS thinking.

Before we ICPS a typical problem among young children—hitting—let's take a look at some of the many responses I've heard parents use over the years. As you read through these *non*-ICPS conversations, see if any sound familiar to you. They point out several ways parents often deal with this problem.

Non-ICPS Conversations About Hitting

CHILD: Bobby hit me.
PARENT: When did he hit you?
CHILD: In school.
PARENT: I'll talk to the teacher about it tomorrow.
> *(In this conversation, the parent solves the problem. The child is not engaged in thinking about the problem at all.)*

In the two conversations below, two mothers give their children different advice about the hitting problem, but they both use the same approach.

CHILD: Amy hit me today.
PARENT: Hit her back.
CHILD: She'd punch me in the nose.
PARENT: Every time she hits you, hit her back. I don't want you to be so timid.
CHILD: But I'm afraid.

PARENT: If you don't learn to defend yourself, kids will keep on hitting you.
CHILD: Okay.

CHILD: Danny knocked me down.
PARENT: What did you do then?
CHILD: I hit him back.
PARENT: You shouldn't hit back. Hitting is not nice. You might hurt someone. It's better to tell the teacher.
CHILD: Then he'll call me a tattletale.
PARENT: If you don't tell the teacher, he'll keep on hitting you.
CHILD: Okay.

> *(These parents ignored their children's views and suggested consequences of their own. One parent told her child what to do; the other, what not to do. But neither child was encouraged to think and decide for him- or herself.)*

When you tell your children how to solve the problem, whether or not your advice is accompanied by explanations, you miss the opportunity to encourage them to offer options of their own. If you insist that one solution is best, as in the above examples, the children are actively discouraged from thinking further about what to do and are left only with worry about how to do what you suggest. With the best of intentions, these parents ignored their children's perception of the problem and never found out why they were hit in the first place.

Sometimes parents do find out why a child was hit, but still are only concerned with what they think the child ought to do. For example:

PARENT: Why did he hit you?
CHILD: I don't know.

PARENT: Did you hit him first, take his toys, or what?
CHILD: I took his book.
PARENT: Are you supposed to take someone else's things?
CHILD: No.
PARENT: What are you supposed to do when you want something?
CHILD: Ask for it.
PARENT: Yes, you should ask. Taking his book is the wrong thing to do. That's why he hit you.
(Still this parent continues to impose her own solution rather than extract one from the child's view.)

Some parents include in their conversation thoughts about other people's feelings. But merely telling children how people feel does not stimulate them to think further about it:

PARENT: Why did Trisha hit you?
CHILD: Her friend told her to.
PARENT: That must have made you angry.
CHILD: Yeah. I'm gonna throw sand in her face.
PARENT: If you do that, she'll get angry, and then you'll have a real fight on your hands. Show her you're a big girl and pay her no mind.
(This parent talks about feelings but is most intent on teaching her child not to hit.)

In all these instances, the advice may differ but the approach is the same: The parent does the thinking for the child. ICPS is different; the ICPS parent guides the child to think about the problem.

An ICPS Dialogue About Hitting

Take a look at this full ICPS dialogue about hitting. To remind you of the purpose of some of the questions, I've pointed out the ICPS process as it appears.

PARENT: Terry, who hit you?
CHILD: Natalie.
PARENT: What happened? Why did she hit you?
(Parent looks for child's view of the problem.)

CHILD: She just hit me.
PARENT: You mean she just hit you for no reason?
(Parent encourages child to think of causes.)

CHILD: Well, I hit her first.
PARENT: What for?
CHILD: She won't let me look at her book.
PARENT: How did Natalie feel when you hit her?
(Parent guides child to think of feelings of others.)

CHILD: Mad.
PARENT: Do you know WHY she doesn't want you to look at her book?
(Parent guides child to appreciate point of view of others.)

CHILD: No.
PARENT: How can you find out?
CHILD: I could ask her.
PARENT: See if you can find out.
(Parent encourages child to seek facts and discover the problem.)
(later)

CHILD: She said I never let her see my books.

PARENT: Now that you know why she said no, can you think of something you could do or say so she'll let you look at her book?

(Parent encourages child to think of solution.)

CHILD: I could stop playing with her.

PARENT: What MIGHT happen if you do that?

(Child is guided to think of consequences of her solution.)

CHILD: She might not be my friend.

PARENT: Do you want her to be your friend?

CHILD: Yes.

PARENT: Can you think of something DIFFERENT to do so she'll still be your friend?

(Parent encourages further solution thinking.)

CHILD: I could let her have one of my books.

PARENT: That's a DIFFERENT idea. Why don't you try that?

When this mother discovered that her child hit first, she didn't offer advice or lecture on the pros and cons of hitting. Instead she continued the ICPS dialogue by encouraging her child to think about Natalie's feelings and the original problem (wanting the book). Then she helped her child look for alternative ways to solve the problem and consider what might happen as a result of those solutions. In the end, it's the child who will solve this problem, not the parent—that's ICPS.

In the ICPS child-child and parent-child dialogues throughout this chapter, you'll find one way in which parents have used the problem-solving approach when a particular problem came up. Once you have a feel for this approach, you will find the process easy to adapt to whichever problem or conflict arises.

Sometimes old habits are hard to break when parents first begin to use ICPS in real problem situations. For example, have you ever heard:

PARENT: Bruce, your teacher tells me you're teasing the other kids and disrupting the class. You're in second grade now and you won't learn anything and you won't have any friends if you keep doing that.
CHILD: I don't care.
PARENT: You're old enough to know better. If you don't stop teasing, I'm going to have to ground you until you do care.
  (*I wonder what's really on the child's mind?*)

Let's try this again—a problem-solving way:

An ICPS Dialogue About Teasing

PARENT: Why do you have to tease the other kids?
CHILD: I don't know.
PARENT: There are probably lots of reasons. IF you think hard, I know you can think of one.
CHILD: Mom, no one likes me.
  (*Oh . . . so* that's *what's on his mind.*)

PARENT: Is teasing the other kids a way to get them to like you?
CHILD: I guess not.
PARENT: What happens when you tease them?
CHILD: Nothing. Well . . . they run away.
PARENT: What can you do so they won't run away?
CHILD: Be their friend?
  (*This parent continued to help the child think*
  through how to be a friend. No more long lectures,
  and now the child cared . . . really cared.)

Principles of Dialoguing Child-Child Problems

There are three basic principles that guide the dialoguing of child-child problems:

1. Find Out the Child's View of the Problem

A power play will develop, and the child's problem won't ever really be solved, if you don't first find out what your child thinks the problem is. If, for example, your child thinks the problem is that he has shared his toy long enough and now simply wants it back, but you think the problem is the grabbing, you'll both be working toward a different goal.

Once you've identified your child's view of the problem, try to resist the temptation to shift the focus of the problem to fit *your* needs. If, for example, a parent realizes that the problem stems from the child's belief that he has shared his toy long enough, but still stays intent on teaching a lesson about sharing, the child will resist finding a solution.

2. Remember That the Child, Not the Adult, Must Solve the Problem

Let your child do the thinking. You should only provide questions that draw out the child's view about what caused the problem, how she and others feel about the situation, her ideas about how to solve the problem, and what she thinks might happen if she were to put the ideas into action. And most important, avoid telling the child what to do or not to do.

3. Focus on the Process of Thinking More Than the Specific Conclusion

The purpose of ICPS is to teach children a style of thinking that will help them deal with interpersonal problems in general. If you put a value judgment on the child's ideas, you stress your view of the problem. Even praising a solution may inhibit further thought about other ideas. And criticism will inhibit the child's willingness to speak out freely about what is on his mind. In any case, the child will shift from thinking about options and consequences to selecting the one thing that gains your approval. This may meet your immediate needs, but it interferes with the thinking process that frees children to ponder the problem and decide for themselves what and what not to do.

◆ ◆ ◆

I know ICPS dialoguing is not always easy to learn; it is a new way to talk with children, and it takes time and practice before it becomes a habit. That's why I've slowly built up each part of the dialogue, chapter by chapter, so you can practice this approach one step at a time before putting it all together.

Also, keep in mind that I'm not suggesting that you use an ICPS dialogue every time you talk with your child; that would be unnatural. But when your child faces a daily problem, you'll find that ICPS talk will come in handy.

More Sample ICPS Dialogues for Child-Child Problems

The following sample dialogues will help you practice ICPS throughout your day so that eventually this process of thinking will become second nature for you and your child.

Being Aggressive

"I Don't Like You."

PARENT: What happened? Why did you kick Mary?
CHILD: I don't like her.

PARENT: How do you think Mary feels when you kick her?
CHILD: Mad.
PARENT: What MIGHT happen IF you kick her?
CHILD: I might hurt her.
PARENT: Can you think of something DIFFERENT to do so you won't hurt Mary and she won't feel ANGRY?
CHILD: I could just stay away from her.
PARENT: That's a DIFFERENT idea. Why don't you try that.

Damaging Property

" 'Cause I'm Mad."

PARENT: Dennis, why did you rip up your sister's book?
CHILD: 'Cause I'm mad at her.
PARENT: Why are you mad at her?
CHILD: 'Cause she called me stupid.
PARENT: What happened?
CHILD: I didn't want to play with her. She's a girl.
PARENT: Did you tell her that?
CHILD: Yep.
PARENT: How do you think Melissa feels when you say things like that?
CHILD: Bad.
PARENT: Do you think that's WHY she called you stupid?
CHILD: Yeah.
PARENT: If you don't want to play with her now, can you think of something else you could say so she won't feel bad and call you names?
CHILD: I could tell her to go away.
PARENT: That's one thing you could say. What MIGHT happen if you say that?
CHILD: She'd probably cry. She's a crybaby.

PARENT: She MIGHT cry. What else could you do or say?
CHILD: I don't know.
PARENT: Okay. You think about that. Now about her book. You ripped it all up. What are you going to do about that?
CHILD: I'll tell her I'm sorry.
PARENT: And what else can you do?
CHILD: Let her have one of mine.
PARENT: Okay. Why don't you try those things and see what happens.

Grabbing

"Give Me That!"

PARENT: What's happening? What's the matter?
CHILD: I want to play with that truck.
PARENT: How do you think Jeffrey feels when you grab from him?
CHILD: Mad. But I don't care. I want it.
PARENT: What did Jeffrey do when you grabbed it?
CHILD: He hit me.
PARENT: How did that make you feel?
CHILD: Mad.
PARENT: So now you're ANGRY and Jeffrey's ANGRY, and he hit you. Can you think of a DIFFERENT way to get a turn to play with the truck so you both won't be ANGRY, and so Jeffrey won't hit you?
CHILD: I could ask him for it.
PARENT: What MIGHT happen if you do that?
CHILD: He'll say no.
PARENT: MAYBE. What else could you do to get the truck?
CHILD: I could trade him my dinosaur.
PARENT: What MIGHT happen IF you do that?
CHILD: I think he'll say okay.
PARENT: Why don't you try that.

Impatience

"I Want to Play Now."

CHILD: Renee won't play with me.
PARENT: How do you know she won't?
CHILD: She said so.
PARENT: What did she say?
CHILD: She wants to read her book.
PARENT: Oh, she wants to do something DIFFERENT NOW.
Maybe she'll play with you when she's finished.
CHILD: But I want to play now.
PARENT: Do you like to play with Renee ALL the time OR
SOME of the time?
CHILD: Some of the time.
PARENT: Do you think Renee can play with you ALL the time?
CHILD: No.
PARENT: Renee is busy now reading her book. Can you think
of something DIFFERENT to do NOW?
CHILD: No.
PARENT: How do you think you would feel IF Renee bothered
you when you were busy?
CHILD: Mad.
PARENT: How do you think Renee will feel if you don't let her
read her book NOW?
CHILD: Mad.
PARENT: IF you can think of something to do NOW, THEN
Renee will not be mad. She really wants to read NOW.
CHILD: I can play with my puzzles.
PARENT: That is something you can do NOW.

Feeling Rejected

"No One Will Play with Me."

CHILD: Robbie and Derek won't let me play.
PARENT: What are they doing?
CHILD: They're cowboys. They chased me away.
PARENT: Do you want to play their game?
CHILD: Yeah.
PARENT: What did you say to them?
CHILD: I'm a cowboy, too.
PARENT: Then what happened?
CHILD: Derek said, "You're too little. You can't play."
PARENT: What did you do then?
CHILD: Nothing.
PARENT: Can you think of something DIFFERENT you can do or say so they will let you play?
CHILD: I can say, "I'm a big cowboy."
PARENT: What MIGHT happen IF you say that?
CHILD: They'll say, "No, you're not."
PARENT: They MIGHT say that. What else can you say or do?
CHILD: I could tell them Indians are coming. I could help catch them.
PARENT: That's a DIFFERENT idea. Try your ideas and see what happens.

Sharing

"He Never Shares."

PARENT: What's the problem?
CHILD: Paul never shares, so I took the crayon from him.
PARENT: What happened after you did that?

CHILD: He cried.
PARENT: And how did Paul feel then?
CHILD: Sad.
PARENT: How do you feel about him not sharing?
CHILD: Mad!
PARENT: Taking is one way to get the crayon. Can you think of something DIFFERENT you can do so he won't be SAD and you won't be ANGRY?
CHILD: I can ask him.
PARENT: That's a DIFFERENT idea. Go ahead and try that.
CHILD: *(to Paul)* Can I have the crayon?
CHILD #2: No.
PARENT: Oh, that idea didn't work. Can you think of a second idea?
CHILD: *(to Paul)* I'll let you play with my new wagon.
CHILD #2: Okay.
PARENT: You thought of a DIFFERENT way. How do you feel about that?

"I Had It First."

PARENT: What's happening?
CHILD #1: I had it first.
CHILD #2: No, I had it first.
PARENT: Sarah, how do you feel when Debbie grabs things from you?
CHILD #1: Mad.
PARENT: Debbie, how do you feel when Sarah grabs things from you?
CHILD #2: Mad.
PARENT: Now you're both mad. Pulling on the doll is one way to get what you want. What happened next when you each pulled on the doll?

CHILD #2: We started fighting.
PARENT: Can either of you think of a DIFFERENT way so you both won't be mad and you won't have to fight?
CHILD #1: We can shake hands.
CHILD #2: We can play together.
PARENT: Why don't you try those ideas?

Summary: Child-Child Problems

Whatever the problem, the questions below form the basis for ICPS dialogues:

1. "What happened?" "What's the matter?" (Sometimes you might want to add, "Because that will help me understand the problem better.")
2. "How does (other child) feel?"
3. "How do you feel?"
4. "Can you think of a different way to solve this problem so you both won't be angry (or so he won't hit you, etc.)?"
5. "Is that a good idea or not a good idea?"
6. (If it's a good idea) "Go ahead and try that."
7. (If it's not good) "Oh, you'll have to think of something different."

Parent-Child Problems

Parent-child problems are ones that occur between you and your child. These are often discipline situations that when handled with the ICPS thinking process quite often eliminate the need for scoldings and punishments.

Sometimes in discipline situations parents forget to ICPS the problem. For example, have you ever heard:

PARENT: Where have you been? I asked you to come right home after school.
CHILD: I forgot.
PARENT: Don't you know I was worried sick?
CHILD: I'm sorry.
PARENT: Don't ever do that again or you're in real trouble! *(This parent is understandably acting out of worry, relief, and exasperation, but in her concern is forgetting about ICPS.)*

Let's try this again, a problem-solving way:

An ICPS Dialogue About Forgetting

PARENT: How do you think I feel when I don't know where you are?
CHILD: Worried, maybe mad.
PARENT: What can you do so I won't worry and I'll know where you are?
CHILD: I could call you. But I was afraid you'd say to come home now.
PARENT: I might have said that. But why do you think I want you to call when I don't know where you are?
CHILD: So you won't worry.
(This child was helped to see beyond his own point of view and to understand that his parents have feelings too.)

Principles of Dialoguing Parent-Child Problems

When you use ICPS to solve problems that occur between your child and yourself, remember these two guidelines:

1. Help Your Child Understand Your Feelings About the Problem

Children need to know why you cannot always satisfy an immediate desire, and why you feel angry when they don't listen, or refuse a request, or break something. Instead of *telling* them how you feel, encourage them to think about your feelings by asking questions like, "Why do you think I can't buy you this toy?" or "Why do you think I get angry when you leave a mess in the living room?"

2. Help Your Child Understand Why the End Goal Is Not Always Going to Be a Choice

Occasionally, your goal in a parenting situation is not negotiable. When you want your child to stop playing and get ready for school, that's the bottom line, and ICPS isn't a platform kids can use to make you change your mind. But even in circumstances where children don't have a choice in the end result, ICPS can lead them to think about how they can get there.

Sometimes your children can use ICPS to think of *how* they'll do what is important to you, and what you value for them. In the case of a messy room, for example, if you want the room cleaned, it's not a question of whether or not the room will be cleaned, but of *how* the room will be cleaned. You can ask your child if he'd like to clean up *all* the toys first and then pick up the clothes *after* dinner. He may choose to stack his toys on the floor in the closet instead of on the shelf up on the wall. ICPS will empower him to think about how to stay within your values of childrearing, but in a way that still gives him some freedom to achieve a given goal.

In other situations, there clearly are no options at all. If you want your child to fasten her seat belt, for example, the question again is not whether or not she will fasten it, but how she thinks about the need to fasten it. ICPS helps you ask questions that can guide her to realize for herself why the belt must be buckled. Now instead of telling her, "Put the belt on because if you don't you might get hurt," you can ask, "What MIGHT happen if you do NOT put the belt on?"

You'll notice in the dialogues below that some use all four dialogue steps, but in others the parent doesn't ask the child, "Can you think of something DIFFERENT to do?" Those are the cases when there are no other viable options. The dialogues merely serve to help the child think about how the problem affects everyone involved.

More Sample ICPS Dialogues for Parent-Child Problems

Bedtime

"I Don't Want to Go to Bed!"

PARENT: Time for bed.
CHILD: I don't want to go to bed!
PARENT: Why do you think you have to go to bed NOW and not LATER?
CHILD: I don't know.
PARENT: What MIGHT happen IF you go to bed LATER?

CHILD: I might be tired tomorrow.
PARENT: What MIGHT happen IF you're tired tomorrow?
CHILD: I won't do good in school.
PARENT: How will you feel IF you wake up tired and don't do well in school?
CHILD: Bad.
PARENT: Is this a GOOD TIME or NOT A GOOD TIME to go to bed?

Buying Toys

"I Want Another One!"

CHILD: I want that truck.
PARENT: What happened to the truck I bought you for your birthday?
CHILD: It got broke—I want another one!
PARENT: How did it break?
CHILD: I took off the wheel.
PARENT: Why did you do that?
CHILD: I wanted to.
PARENT: How do think I feel when I pay good money to buy you toys and you just break them like that?
CHILD: Mad.
PARENT: Do you think you deserve this truck?
CHILD: Yes.
PARENT: Why?
CHILD: 'Cause I want it.
PARENT: What can you do to get me to buy you another truck?
CHILD: Not break it.
PARENT: How can I know you won't break it?
CHILD: I won't break any more of my toys.
PARENT: Are you going to play with them the SAME way or a DIFFERENT way?

CHILD: A different way.
PARENT: How are you going to play with them?
CHILD: I won't take the wheels off and I won't throw them.
PARENT: Okay. When you show me you won't break your toys, we'll talk about this truck again.

"Can I Have . . ."

CHILD: Can I have this talking doll?
PARENT: Erica, you know I have to take you with me every time I go shopping. What MIGHT happen to all my money IF I bought you toys that cost a lot every time you wanted them?
CHILD: You wouldn't have no more money.
PARENT: Yes, that MIGHT happen.
CHILD: Can I have this? *(picks out a little trinket)*
PARENT: Yes, you can have that. That doesn't cost much.

Cleaning

"Do I Have to?"

PARENT: JoAnn, I asked you to clean your room but it's still a mess.
CHILD: Oh, do I have to?
PARENT: How do you think I feel when you leave your room so messy?
CHILD: Mad.
PARENT: Do you know why it makes me feel mad?
CHILD: 'Cause you always tell me to clean it up?
PARENT: Yes, but do you know why I want your room to be clean?
CHILD: I don't know.

PARENT: Well, try to guess. Can you think of any reason I would like your room to be clean?

CHILD: Because you like things to look nice?

PARENT: That's one reason. Can you think of a DIFFERENT reason?

CHILD: Because when it's clean you can walk across the room without stepping on stuff?

PARENT: Yes. And how do you feel when your room is clean?

CHILD: I like it.

"Make Him Help Me!"

PARENT: Dorothy, were you playing with these toys?

CHILD: Brian played too.

PARENT: Did you and Brian play together?

CHILD: Yes.

PARENT: Is it FAIR for Brian to pick them up by himself and for you NOT to pick them up at all?

CHILD: No.

PARENT: Is it FAIR for you to pick them ALL up and NOT Brian?

CHILD: No.

PARENT: What IS FAIR?

CHILD: Brian should help but he won't.

PARENT: Can you think of a way to get Brian to help you pick up the toys?

CHILD: I could ask him.

PARENT: That's one idea. What MIGHT happen IF you do that?

CHILD: He'll say no.

PARENT: That MIGHT happen. What else can you think of to do IF he says no?

CHILD: Hit him.

PARENT: You could hit him. What MIGHT happen then?

CHILD: We'll fight.

PARENT: MAYBE you'd fight. Can you think of a third, DIF-FERENT idea?

CHILD: You could make him help me.

PARENT: I could make him, but that won't help you when I'm not here. Can you think of a DIFFERENT way?

CHILD: I could say I won't play with him anymore.

PARENT: Is that a good idea?

CHILD: Yeah.

PARENT: WHY?

CHILD: 'Cause then he'll help me.

PARENT: MAYBE. Why don't you give that a try.

Eating

"I'm Not Hungry."

PARENT: What's the matter? Why aren't you eating?

CHILD: I'm not hungry.

PARENT: WHY aren't you hungry?

CHILD: I don't know.

PARENT: Did you eat cookies just a little while ago?

CHILD: Yes, 'cause I was hungry.

PARENT: How do you think I feel when you eat cookies BE-FORE dinner and then don't eat this good food?

CHILD: Mad.

PARENT: How do you think your body feels when it doesn't get good food?

CHILD: Sick?

PARENT: It MIGHT. What can you do so I won't feel angry and your body won't feel sick?

CHILD: How about if I eat just some of this food?

PARENT: You MIGHT do that. What else might you do the next time?

CHILD: I won't eat cookies before supper.

"I Don't Like Vegetables."

PARENT: What's the matter? Why aren't you eating your carrots?

CHILD: I don't like vegetables.

PARENT: I thought you did; you eat carrots for a snack all the time.

CHILD: But those aren't cooked and gushy like these.

PARENT: Well, can you think of something to do so you do eat a vegetable with dinner?

CHILD: I could eat one from the refrigerator that's not cooked.

PARENT: Is that a good solution?

CHILD: Yeah, because hard carrots still have good stuff in 'em.

PARENT: Okay. Raw carrots are still vegetables.

Irresponsible Behavior

"I Forgot."

PARENT: Cheryl, didn't I ask you to pick up your toys?

CHILD: I forgot.

PARENT: Is the middle of the floor a good place to leave your toys?

CHILD: No.

PARENT: What MIGHT happen IF you leave them there?

CHILD: Someone might fall on them.

PARENT: And then what MIGHT happen?

CHILD: They might get hurt?

PARENT: How will we all feel IF someone gets hurt?

CHILD: Sad—and mad.

PARENT: Can you think of a DIFFERENT place to put these toys so no one will fall on them, and no one will get hurt?

CHILD: I can put them in my room.
PARENT: Good thinking. You can decide where in your room you want to put them.

Lying

"He Did It."

PARENT: Jessica, what happened? How did this vase break?
CHILD: Keith did it.
PARENT: Oh, do you know how it happened?
CHILD: He ran into it.
PARENT: *(knowing differently)* I'll have to talk to him. I'm really hurt that he wasn't more careful.
CHILD: Mommy, I did it. Don't yell at Keith.
PARENT: Why did you tell me that Keith did it?
CHILD: I was afraid.
PARENT: I see. Tell me how it happened.
CHILD: I knocked it off.
PARENT: What were you doing?
CHILD: Playing.
PARENT: Were you playing near the vase?
CHILD: Yes.
PARENT: I'm glad you told me the truth. What can you do about this now?
CHILD: I can help you find a new one.
PARENT: Yes, you can do that. What are you going to think about next time you're playing near something that can break?
CHILD: I'm not going to play there.

Nagging for Attention

"Read to Me Now."

CHILD: Will you read me this story?

PARENT: I'm busy making supper right NOW. When I get this in the oven, then I can read to you.

CHILD: Why can't you read it now?

PARENT: BECAUSE I want to eat supper at six and this food has to go into the oven NOW. Can you think of something DIFFERENT to do until I finish?

CHILD: No.

PARENT: You're just teasing me. What can you think of to do?

CHILD: I'll look at the pictures in the book.

PARENT: That's one thing you can do.

CHILD: Then I'll watch TV.

PARENT: You thought of two things to do. If you still want me to read the story when I'm finished, tell me. Okay?

CHILD: Okay.

Damaging Property

"I Won't Spill It."

PARENT: What MIGHT happen IF you play with water in the living room?

CHILD: Nothing. I won't spill it.

PARENT: MAYBE you won't spill it, but what else MIGHT happen?

CHILD: Well, it might spill.

PARENT: And how would I feel if you spilled water in here?

CHILD: Mad.

PARENT: WHY do you think I'd be mad?

CHILD: 'Cause it would make a mess on the rug.

PARENT: Can you think of a DIFFERENT place to play with water so you won't spill it?

CHILD: In the sink.

PARENT: Is that a good place?

CHILD: Yeah, 'cause the water goes down the sink.

PARENT: And can you think of a second, DIFFERENT place that's good?

CHILD: Outside.

PARENT: You can choose to play with water in either of those places.

Traveling

"Stop Kicking Me."

CHILD #1: Make him stop kicking me.

CHILD #2: Oh, stop being such a baby. I'm not doing anything to you.

PARENT: How do you think I feel when I'm trying to drive the car and you two keep fighting?

CHILD #1: Mad.

PARENT: What MIGHT happen IF I keep turning around to stop your fighting?

CHILD #2: You could get into an accident.

PARENT: How would you feel if I got into an accident BE-CAUSE of your fighting?

CHILD #2: Bad.

PARENT: What can you do so I won't feel ANGRY and I won't get into an accident?

"I Don't Want to Wear a Seat Belt."

PARENT: Put on your seat belt.
CHILD: I don't want to.
PARENT: Why don't you want to wear a seat belt?
CHILD: 'Cause I don't like it.
PARENT: Why do you think you have to wear it?
CHILD: 'Cause if we get in an accident I'd get hurt.
PARENT: How do you think you'd feel IF we got in an accident and you got hurt BECAUSE you didn't have your seat belt on?
CHILD: Sad and hurt.

Idea, Time, or Place Problems

During each day children frequently become involved in activities as commonplace as running in the house that are not a good idea, or at a good time, or in a good place. You can often avoid potential problems by using ICPS in those circumstances to help your children think about their actions. Have you ever heard:

PARENT: Linwood, don't tie your rope across the doorway! No one will be able to get in or out.
CHILD: I'm sorry.
PARENT: What's the matter with you? You know that's not a good place to play with a rope.
   (This parent explained the consequences, but didn't help Linwood identify the potential problem.)

Let's try this again, a problem-solving way:

PARENT: Linwood, is that a good place to tie your rope?
CHILD: I guess not.

PARENT: What MIGHT happen IF you keep the rope stretched across the doorway?

CHILD: Nobody can get into the house.

PARENT: How MIGHT people feel IF they can't get in?

CHILD: Mad.

PARENT: Can you think of a different place to tie your rope?

CHILD: On the door in my room.

> *(Linwood's motive wasn't to keep people from going in and out of the house. He wanted only to practice tying ropes. This mom no longer scolded her son for something he hadn't intended at all.)*

More Sample ICPS Dialogues for Idea, Time, or Place Problems

Once your children are in the habit of ICPS thinking, you'll find that you won't even need to use a full dialogue. One morning, for example, Eddie put his hand in the bowl where his mother was using the egg-beater to prepare breakfast. His mom stopped whipping and asked, "Is that a good place for your hand?" Eddie, adopting the ICPS style of thinking, replied, "No, because I might get hurt," and took his hand away from the bowl. Eddie's mom didn't need a full ICPS dialogue that included feelings, solutions, and consequences. Eddie knew. To quickly remind your children to use ICPS thinking, you can ask the same two or three questions in a variety of circumstances:

When a Child Is Drawing on the Wall (Table, Floor, etc.)

"Is that a good place to draw?"

"WHY is that NOT a good place?"

"Where IS a good place to draw?"

When a Child Is Leaving Toys in an Unsafe Place

"Is that a good place for the toy?"

"Where IS a good place?"

When a Child Won't Dress Properly for Cold Weather

"Is going out in the snow without your boots on a good idea?"

"WHY NOT? BECAUSE _____."

"What else do you need to put on when you go out in the snow?"

When a Child Runs Through the House

"Is it a good idea to run in the house?"

"What MIGHT happen IF you run inside?"

"Can you think of something DIFFERENT to do while you're inside?"

When a Child Interrupts

"Is this a GOOD TIME to talk to me?"

"Can I talk to you AND to _____ at the SAME time?"

"What can you do while you wait?"

When a Child Is Painting in Good Clothes

"Is it a good idea to paint in your good clothes?"

"What MIGHT happen IF you paint in your good clothes?"

"What can you do so your clothes will NOT *(repeat what child says)?*"

When a Child Is Riding a Bicycle Too Fast

"Is riding fast a good idea?"

"What MIGHT happen IF you ride too fast?"

"Can you think of a DIFFERENT way to ride that bike?"

When a Child Is Holding Scissors Incorrectly

"Is that a good way to hold your scissors while you're walking?"

"Can you think of a DIFFERENT way to hold your scissors?"

When a Child Is Standing Too Close to Other Children Playing Ball

"Is that a good place to stand?"

"Can you think of a DIFFERENT place to stand?"

When a Child's Feet Are on the Furniture

"Is that a good place for your feet?"

"Can you think of a DIFFERENT place to put your feet?"

When Children Are Playing in Front of a Doorway

"Is that a good place to play?"

"Can you think of a DIFFERENT place to play?"

When a Child Calls Another Child a Name

"Is that a good idea?"

"How do you think he feels when you do that?"

"What MIGHT happen next?"

Good time, good place, good idea. Once your children understand ICPS thinking, you can ask just two or three ICPS questions and avoid a long list of potential problems. These questions also help your children practice consequential thinking—soon you may even hear your little problem solver show off his or her thinking skills among friends. That's what happened several months after Marie brought ICPS into her home. One evening she overheard her four-year-old Alex yell out to one of his friends, "That's not a good place to leave your bike 'cause it might get run over by a car."

"Well," thought Marie, "now Alex really is an ICPS kid."

COMMON PROBLEMS

Between Child and Child

Between Parent and Child

Epilogue

Over the last twenty-five years I have seen how ICPS has benefited children in schools throughout the country and how parents have enjoyed taking it from the schools into their own homes. Now I'm delighted to have this chance to come directly into your home. I hope that ICPS will help you in your challenging task of raising children in a society where some have forgotten how to think first and act second. Is it too presumptuous of me to predict that if the next generation of adolescents and adults are ICPS thinkers, then perhaps this country will become a more compassionate and humane place for our children and their children to live?

APPENDIX A

♦ ● ♦

Self-Evaluation Checklist

Every once in a while, you might want to ask yourself, "How am I doing?" ICPS skills are the kind that you want to use continually with your children in the years to come, and yet it's likely that you'll sometimes forget ICPS, telling them how to solve a problem rather than letting them think about how to solve it themselves. The following checklist is a handy and quick way to evaluate how well you're using ICPS skills.

If you find yourself answering "yes" to statements 1, 2, and 3, you probably still need more practice using ICPS dialogues that encourage your child to think about a problem rather than listen to you tell him about it. When you can check off statement 4, you're well on your way to becoming an ICPS parent.

Today (or this week) when I spoke to my children, I:

1. was demanding, commanding, and/or belittling.

   EXAMPLES:

   "Sit down!"

   "You can't do that!"

   "You know you shouldn't _____!"

   "How many times have I told you _____?"

2. offered suggestions without explanations.

EXAMPLES:

"You can't go around hitting kids."

"Why don't you ask him for it?"

"Children must learn to share."

3. offered suggestions with explanations, including talk of feelings.

EXAMPLES:

"IF you hit, you MIGHT lose a friend."

"IF you grab, she won't let you play with her toys."

"You shouldn't do that. It's NOT FAIR."

"You'll make him ANGRY IF you do that."

4. guided my child to think of feelings, solutions, consequences.

EXAMPLES:

"What's the problem?"

"How do you think your friend feels when _____?"

"What MIGHT happen IF _____?"

"What can you do so that will NOT happen?"

"Do you think that IS or IS NOT a good idea?"

"Can you think of a DIFFERENT way?"

├──────────────┤

◆ ● ◆

For You and Your Child: Things to Think About

While your children are learning to ICPS, you'll find that you will begin to reevaluate the way you relate to them. The following exercises are a fun way to help you think about the special relationship between you and your children.

Points of View

Happy, Sad, Angry

1. What does your child do or say to make you feel:

    happy?
    sad?
    angry?

2. Why does (your answer to question 1) make you feel:

    happy?
    sad?
    angry?

3. What do *you* do or say that might make your child feel:

happy?
sad?
angry?

4. Why might (your answer to question 3) make your child feel:

happy?
sad?
angry?

A Time When . . .

Can you think of a time when:

1. you and your child felt the SAME way about something?
2. you and your child felt DIFFERENT ways about the SAME thing?
3. you thought your child liked something that he or she did NOT?
4. your child thought you liked something that you did NOT?
5. you found out what your child liked by *seeing* what he or she was doing?
6. you found out what your child liked by *hearing* what he or she said?
7. you found out what your child liked by *asking*?

More Points of View

Proud, Frustrated
Think of a time when:

1. you felt PROUD of your child.
2. you felt PROUD of yourself.

3. you think your child felt PROUD of him- or herself.
4. you think your child was PROUD of you. (How could you tell she or he felt that way?)
5. you felt FRUSTRATED with your child.
6. you felt FRUSTRATED about something yourself.
7. you think your child felt FRUSTRATED. (How could you tell your child felt that way?)
8. you think your child felt FRUSTRATED with you. (How could you tell your child felt that way?)

Good Time/Not Good Time

Think of a time when:

1. your child picked a NOT GOOD TIME to ask to do something; for example, when you were:

busy
tired
sick
in a bad mood

2. your child waited for a GOOD TIME to ask you to do something.
3. you picked a NOT GOOD TIME to ask your child to do something.

Different Ways: Actual Problem

The purpose of this activity is to learn more about using ICPS talk with your child.

Think about an actual problem situation you had to deal with recently with your child.

1. What was the first thing you actually said or did when the problem came up?

2. What happened next? What was the very next thing your child said or did when you did (or said) that?
3. What did you do or say next?

Continue thinking about everything that was actually said or done from the time the problem first came up to when it was resolved.

Now think about the following:

1. Did you get all the facts from your child?
2. Did you find out how he or she felt when the problem came up? (How did you find out?)
3. Can you think of another way you might have handled the same problem? Something else you might have said or done when your child said (or did) that?

Finding Out

Quiz yourself periodically on how ICPS is working for you as a parent. Ask yourself if you can think of a time when:

1. you recognized a problem with your child:

   by seeing but not hearing or asking.
   by hearing but not seeing or asking.
   by asking but not seeing or hearing.
   by two or all three of these ways.

2. you learned something you didn't know about your child through ICPS dialoguing.
3. your child was having a problem and you thought you knew what the problem was, but after using ICPS dialoguing you found out it was actually something quite different.

APPENDIX C

|————————|
◆ ● ◆

ICPS Reminders

You might want to copy these child-child and parent-child dialogue reminders and hang them in a visible place such as on your refrigerator. When real problems arise during your day, they will help you remember how to talk with your children the ICPS way. Of course, they are only guidelines, but they can prompt you to use this new approach.

Child-Child Problems

"What happened?" "What's the Matter?"

"How does _____ feel?"

"How do *you* feel?"

"What happened when you did that?"

"How did that make *you* feel?"

"Can you think of a DIFFERENT way
to solve this problem (so you both won't
be angry, he won't hit you, etc.)?"

"Is that a GOOD IDEA or
NOT A GOOD IDEA?"

If good idea: "Go ahead and try that."
If not good: "Oh, you'll have to think
of something DIFFERENT."

Parent-Child Problems

"Can I talk to you AND to
_____ at the SAME TIME?"

"Is this a GOOD TIME to talk to me?
(to _____)?"

"Can you think of a GOOD TIME to talk
to me? (to _____)?"

"Is that a GOOD PLACE to draw,
leave food, stand, etc.?"

"Can you think of a GOOD PLACE
to _____ ?"

"How do you think *I* feel when you
don't listen, throw food, interrupt me?"

"Can you think of something DIFFERENT
to do NOW until (you can fingerpaint,
I can help you, etc.)?"

Selected References

Classroom Manuals (for use by teachers and other school personnel)

Shure, M. B. *I Can Problem Solve (ICPS): An Interpersonal Cognitive Problem Solving Program* [preschool]. Champaign, Ill: Research Press, 1992.

———. *I Can Problem Solve (ICPS): An Interpersonal Cognitive Problem Solving Program* [kindergarten/primary grades]. Champaign, Ill: Research Press, 1992.

———. *I Can Problem Solve (ICPS): An Interpersonal Cognitive Problem Solving Program* [intermediate elementary grades]. Champaign, Ill: Research Press, 1992.

Books and Periodicals

Cheek, J. M., A. M. Carpentieri, T. G. Smith, J. Rierdan, and E. Koff. "Adolescent Shyness." In *Shyness: Perspectives on Research and Treatment,* edited by W. H. Jones, J. M. Cheek, and S. R. Briggs, pp. 105–15. New York: Plenum Press, 1986.

Parker, J. G., and S. R. Asher. "Peer Relations and Later Personal Adjustment: Are Low-accepted Children at Risk?" *Psychological Bulletin* 102 (1987): 357–89.

Shure, M. B. "How to Think, Not What to Think: A Cognitive Approach to Prevention." In *Families in Transition: Primary*

Prevention Programs That Work, edited by L. A. Bond and B. M. Wagner, 170–99. Beverly Hills, Calif.: Sage, 1988.

————. *Interpersonal Problem Solving and Prevention*. A comprehensive report of research and training. #MH-40801. Washington, D.C.: National Institute of Mental Health, 1993.

————. "Solving Everyday Problems: A New Approach to Promoting Healthy Behaviors in Children." In *Channeling Children's Anger: Proceedings of the International Invitational Conference on Children and the Media*, edited by R. Baruch and P. Vesin, 199–226. Sponsored by the Institute of Mental Health Initiatives, Washington, D.C., and Centre International de L'Enfance, Paris, 1988.

Shure, M. B., and G. Spivack. "Interpersonal Cognitive Problem Solving." In *14 Ounces of Prevention: A Casebook for Practitioners*, edited by R. H. Price, E. L. Cowen, R. P. Lorion, and J. Ramos-McKay, 69–82. Washington, D.C.: American Psychological Association, 1988.

————. "Interpersonal Problem Solving in Young Children: A Cognitive Approach to Prevention." *American Journal of Community Psychology* (Special issue on primary prevention, Emory Cowen, guest editor) 10 (1982): 341–56.

————. "Interpersonal Problem-Solving Thinking and Adjustment in the Mother-Child Dyad." In *The Primary Prevention of Psychopathology*, Vol. 3: *Social Competence in Children*, edited by M. W. Kent and J. E. Rolf, Hanover, N.H.: University Press of New England, 1979.

Spivack, G., and M. B. Shure. "Interpersonal Cognitive Problem-Solving and Clinical Theory." In *Advances in Child Clinical Psychology*. Vol. 5, edited by B. Lahey and A. E. Kazdin, 323–72. New York: Plenum Press, 1982.

Index

Schneider, Nimisha
Thu Feb 11 2016

EMAIL

p22228871

Hello Ruby : adventures in coding / Linda
Liukas.
31189930789239

Brookline Main